D1507794

© 2002 by Dee Wampler. All rights reserved.
2nd edition 2004.

Published by WinePress Publishing, PO Box 428, Enumclaw, WA 98022.

No part of this publication may be reproduced, stored in a retrieval system or transmitted in any way by any means, electronic, mechanical, photocopy, recording or otherwise, without the prior permission of the copyright holder except as provided by USA copyright law.

Unless otherwise noted, all Scriptures are taken from the Holy Bible, New International Version, Copyright © 1973, 1978, 1984 by the International Bible Society. Used by permission of Zondervan Publishing House. The "NIV" and "New International Version" trademarks are registered in the United States Patent and Trademark Office by International Bible Society.

ISBN 1-57921-623-4
Library of Congress Catalog Card Number: 2003116995

 *Our forefathers made a covenant with God and dedicated this land to the Lord.*

Most everyone thinks there is a separation of church and state. They are wrong.
There never has been; there isn't now.
Most think it is in the Constitution. It isn't.

Most are afraid to question the subject; they don't want to offend anyone. Christians especially want to avoid making anyone mad. You know, turn the other cheek; that sort of thing. Remember, don't offend, don't correct. And whatever you do, don't speak out as a Christian or people will make fun of you. Stop mentioning Jesus in public conversations! You'll turn people off.

Even though our founding fathers said America is a Christian nation, their remarks have been erased from most of our history books. It is little wonder we are confused because historical revisionists have tried to change our past. Some commonly understood lies which abound in our nation today include:

1. The check is in the mail.
2. I'm from the government and I'm here to help you.
3. Our constitution requires a total wall of separation between church and state.

This book is about one of those myths. It is a collection of thoughts of our founders who were some of the most thoughtful men and women that ever lived in our nation. There is a vision of greatness and dedication to their high purpose. Their words instruct and inspire. Americans should be proud to possess the world's longest-lasting and most imitated written political document in the *Constitution*. John Adams said:

"Human passions unbridled by morality and religion . . . would break the strongest cords of our Constitution as a whale goes through a net. Our people must possess the right dispositions, strong, but tempered religious beliefs, to keep what our Founders have bequeathed them."

Our Founders thought virtues as essential for the success of America. We have lost the art of moral education. We must teach our children piety, religion, morality, and virtue. As John Hancock marveled, the Lord gave this country:

"... name and a standing among the nations of the world ... I hope and pray that the gratitude of their hearts may be expressed by proper use of those inestimable blessings, by the greatest exertions of patriotism, by forming and supporting institutions for cultivating the human understanding, and for the greatest progress of the Arts and Sciences, by establishing laws for the support of piety, religion, and morality ..."

Americans should be worried about the source of our present discontent-moral decline. We have fallen short of our duties and aspirations. As novelist Tom Wolfe stated:

"We need a great re-learning. We need to restore this nation's sense of greatness, to learn once again about the great deeds and the great men and women of our past so that we might move forward in the long journey towards moral reform and cultural renaissance in America."

Of course, our founding fathers certainly were not angels and often did not live by their own advice. If men were angels, there would be no need for government. But their flaws, whether great or small, would hardly disqualify them to be used as guides to us today.

Their remarks have been removed from most of our history books. Historical revisionists have erased their repeated references to and reliance upon God. There has never been a separation of church and state in our nation. There never will be. It is not in our law now and was never intended to be a part of our law from the very beginning of our nation. There is an accommodation between the two, a close one that is permanent and longstanding.

❖

John Adams urged Americans of his time to, "Read and recollect and impress upon our souls the views and ends of our own immediate forefathers," and, "Recollect their amazing fortitude."

Let's start now by setting the record straight.

July 4, 2004

Dee Wampler
Attorney at Law
2974 E. Battlefield
Springfield, Missouri 65804

OUR PAST

"There is no solid basis for a civilization but in the Word of God. If we abide by the principles taught in the Bible, our country will go on prospering and to prosper. Our ancestors established their system of government on morality and religious sentiment. Moral habits, they believed, cannot safely be trusted on any other foundation than religious principle, nor any government be secure which is not supported by moral habits . . . whatever makes men good Christians, makes them good citizens."

—Daniel Webster
December 22, 1820

"Let all the earth fear the Lord: let all the inhabitants of the world stand in awe of him. For he spake, and it was done; he commanded, and it stood fast . . . the counsel of the Lord stands forever . . . blessed is the nation whose God is the Lord: and the people whom he has chosen for his own inheritance.

—Psalm 33: 8–12

"Columbus was not the kind of man to take no for an answer. He was sure he could do it, certain that God meant him to do it; his name meant "Christ bearer" so he was destined to carry the good tidings to heathen lands. The only solid thing about it was his faith in God and his mission."

—The Oxford History of the American People

From the beginning, European believers took a religious interest in America. In his very first entry in the diary that recorded his journey to America in 1492, Christopher Columbus expressed hope he would make contact with native peoples in order to find out "the manner in which may be undertaken their conversion to our holy faith."

On his second journey in 1493, Columbus brought Catholic friars with the hope they could convert the Indians he had seen on his first voyage. To the Spanish monarchs, Columbus insisted profits from his voyages be used to restore Christian control over Jerusalem.

Columbus had a very high sense of divine calling. In a lengthy manuscript penned after his third voyage, a Book of Prophecies, he recorded the many passages from Scripture he felt related to his mission to the East Indies.

America: the Promised Land

America's founders saw our nation in a biblically spiritual light. The Pilgrims viewed America as divinely chosen by God, much as the ancient Israelites saw the land of Canaan as they came to it from Egypt.

The American concept of the Promised Land was not confined to Pilgrims but referred to throughout the nation's history by Benjamin Franklin, John Adams, Thomas Jefferson, and many others. At Jefferson's urging, the Continental Congress appointed a special committee to design a seal of the United States of America. The sketch portrayed Americans, like the Children of Israel, being led by a cloud during the day and a pillar of fire by night in pursuit of the Promised Land.

The Pilgrims and prominent Americans thereafter believed God providentially led them to the Promised Land and also preserved it for them. The extraordinary, fortuitous events that occurred during our war of independence, from a military perspective, indicate that America should have never won the war. Many Americans, including George Washington, believe God intervened to save the nation. When the Americans took Boston without a single casualty, Washington recognized the hand of God calling it a "remarkable introposition of Providence."[1]

Washington's heralded success in crossing the Delaware River in the predawn hours of Christmas Day, 1776, was yet another time when a violent storm, creating near zero visibility, made it impossible for the British sentries to see Washington's flotilla

George Washington

coming in to attack. The British soldiers (Hessians) were caught off-guard, and in less than an hour the battle was over. General Henry Knox (one of Washington's military experts) wrote that, "Providence seemed to have smiled upon every part of this enterprise."[2]

At the Battle of Princeton in January, 1777, Washington rode a highly visible white horse, making him a conspicuous and easy target for the British who were only yards away. Soldiers fell and died all around him, but Washington sat solidly on his horse, untouched.

At the Battle of the Monongahela near Fort Duquesne (now Pittsburgh), Washington had two horses killed under him and four bullet holes ripped through his coat.[3]

In these and many other experiences, Washington and other leaders recognized God's intervening action. These examples of prominent Americans who believed God had providentially preserved the nation in some of its most critical hours in history does not sit well with multiculturalists and carries far too much Judeo-Christian freight.[4]

It is not known exactly what Benjamin Franklin meant when he answered the question, "What kind of government are you going to have?" with, "A republic, if you can keep it,"[5] he believed a republican government could endure only if its leaders and people were given to moral virtues. They needed to obey God's moral laws—a quality that the republic of Ancient Rome sadly lacked.

Columbus attending first religious ceremonies

Thomas Jefferson said, "I think that our government will remain virtuous."[6]

Benjamin Rush believed:

"The only foundation for a useful education in a republic is to be laid in Religion. Without this, there would be no virtue, and without virtue there can be no liberty, and liberty is the object and life of all republican governments."[7]

Our founders believed we could endure only if our people lived honest, morally upright lives. If the practice of virtue gives way to moral and cultural relativism, as multiculturalism espouses, Americans (according to Franklin, Rush, and others) would lose their republic, their freedom, and the blessings that their once Promised Land bestowed.

To jettison our nation's longstanding moral norms such as the Ten Commandments, which have been the foundation of American virtue from our nation's beginning, would be to reject our past. It is little wonder that Americans today are experiencing a moral meltdown, a culture creep. If our country's highest leaders live as though there is no moral law, no God, and no sense of shame, and if the Ten Commandments are erased from America's schools and public buildings and disappear from the people's convictions, then America's soul is on the precipice.

Christopher Columbus (1451–1506)

"Neither reason nor mathematics . . . nor world maps were profitable to me; rather the prophecy of Isaiah was completely fulfilled."

Before his fleet set sail August 2, 1492, every man and boy confessed his sins and received absolution and communion.

Columbus won the support of Queen Isabella of Castille and King Ferdinand of Aragon, and after the longest voyage ever made out of sight of *Christopher Columbus* land, discovered the New World on October 12, 1492. Then Columbus wrote, according to his diary:

"At a very early age I began to sail upon the ocean. For more than forty years, I have sailed everywhere that people go.

I prayed to the most merciful Lord about my heart's great desire, and He gave me the spirit and the intelligence for the task: seafaring, astronomy, geometry, arithmetic, skill in drafting spherical maps and placing correctly the cities, rivers, mountains and ports. I also studied cosmology, history, chronology, and philosophy.

It was the Lord who put into my mind (I could feel His hand upon me) the fact that it would be possible to sail from here to the Indies. All who heard of my project rejected it with laughter, ridiculing me.

There is no question that the inspiration was from the Holy Spirit, because He comforted me with rays of marvelous illumination from the Holy Scriptures, a strong and clear testimony from the 44 books of the Old Testament, from the four Gospels, and from the 23 Epistles of the blessed Apostles, encouraging me continually to press forward, and without ceasing for a moment they now encourage me to make haste.

Our Lord Jesus desired to perform a very obvious miracle in the voyage to the Indies, to comfort me and the whole people of God . . .

Landing of Columbus

I am a most unworthy sinner, but I have cried out to the Lord for grace and mercy, and they have covered me completely. I have found the sweetest consolations since I made it my whole purpose to enjoy His marvelous presence.

For the execution of this journey to the Indies, I did

not make use of intelligence, mathematics, or maps. It is simply the fulfillment of what Isaiah had prophesied.

All this is what I desire to write down for you in this book.

No one should fear to undertake any task in the name of our Savior, if it is just and if the intention is purely for His holy service. The working out of all things has been assigned to each person by our Lord, but it all happens according to His sovereign will even though He gives advice.

Christopher Columbus

He lacks nothing that it is in the power of men to give him. Oh, what a gracious Lord, who desires that people should perform for Him those things for which He holds Himself responsible! Day and night, moment by moment, everyone should express to Him their most devoted gratitude.

I said that some of the prophecies remained yet to be fulfilled. These are great and wonderful things for the earth, and the signs are that the Lord is hastening the end. The fact that the gospel must still be preached to so many lands in such a short time, this is what convinces me."[8]

When a seaman on the Pinta gave the "Land ho!" and everyone thought he saw an island against the setting sun, Columbus fell on his knees to thank God, and ordered, GLORIA, in EXCELCIS DEO! to be sung by all.

Although Columbus did not land until days later, he continued to give praise and insisted that his route was directed . . . with "the help of our Lord."[9] Columbus frequently wrestled with God to find out why some things turned out badly for him. He performed religious duties regularly and did his best to convert the Indians to the True Faith.[10]

Of course, Columbus may have had a zealous belief in his own messianic mission, and the way he and his subordinates treated Native Americans was anything but Christian. Mixed reactions to Columbus' Christian mission are, not surprisingly, prevalent. To many Catholic ethnic groups he was a hero, the first of a host of self-sacrificing, faithful missionaries. To the National Council of Churches (1990), he bears significant responsibility for genocide, slavery and the exploitation of the wealth of the land.

The Cape Henry Landing

Three tiny sailing ships—the Susan Constance, the Godspeed, and the Discovery—rode at anchor at Chesapeake Bay, just off Cape Henry, Virginia. Most of the 149 men of the Virginia Company lined the railings, squinting into the late afternoon sun.

They waited for the return of Captain John Smith's scouting party before they clambered down rope ladders off their small ships after a 4,000 mile journey from England to America.

As the Forefathers disembarked and were being ferried to the beach at Cape Henry, Captain John Smith, his soldiers, and the ship's carpenter erected in the sand a rough wooden cross they had carried from England just for this day.

They had survived 130 days in a crowded, cold, and foul-smelling hold in the darkness beneath the deck. Now they stood on wobbly legs in the fabled New World. The exhausted, lonely, and dispirited crowd noticed their chaplain, Reverend Robert Hunt, wading towards them wearing a silver cross around his neck and carrying a rare, much treasured Bible in his hands. Hunt led a public prayer for the first permanent settlement in America. Together, the men of the Virginia Company thanked God for their safe journey and re-committed themselves to His plan and purpose for the New World.

The Mayflower Compact

In the name of God, Amen!

The *Mayflower Compact*, written November 11, 1620, was America's first great governmental document. It was signed by the Pilgrims before they disembarked their ship, the *Mayflower*.

This covenant was so revolutionary and it has influenced every other constitutional instrument written since its time in America.

Beginning with the words "In the name of God, Amen!" it was the very first contract and government document ever entered into in our nation.[11]

The group of Separationists-Puritans who had seceded from the Church of England sailed the Mayflower on a rough voyage of 64 days to Cape Cod. On December 16, the Mayflower began landing passengers. With the help of a friendly Indian, they learned how to plant and cultivate corn. Miles Standish taught them to shoot game; fish, clams, and lobsters were plentiful. In October, they invited friendly Wampanoag Indians to share their first Thanksgiving feast.[12]

The similarities between the *Mayflower Compact* and a church covenant are striking. God is called upon as witness. The colonists notify any future readers that they wish to become a people who glorify God, advance the Christian religion, honor king and country, and value justice, equality, and the common good.[13]

On November 15, 1636, the Pilgrim "Code of Law" was signed. We see a free, self-governing people using a deliberate process based upon their consent and focused upon a representative assembly beholden to a virtuous people as measured by God's law.[14]

The leaders undertook the voyage "for the glorie of God, and advancemente of ye Christ faith and honour of our king and countrie," according to William Bradford, reported the landing of the Mayflower passengers:

> "They fell upon their knees and blessed the God of heaven who had brought them over the vast and furious ocean, and delivered them from all the perils and miseries thereof . . ."[15]

The *Arbella* landed in the spring of 1630 with the future leaders of the Massachusetts Bay Colony. John Winthrop, preaching to fellow passengers, stated:

> "We shall be as a City upon a Hill, the eyes of all the people are upon us; so that if we shall deal falsely with our god in this work, we have undertaken and so cause him to withdraw his present help from us we shall be made a story and by-word through the world."[16]

The *Mayflower Compact* was the antecedent of our *Declaration of Independence* and *Constitution*, and reveals a wealth of evidence and opinion as the first written political and social contract in the New World. It was an inspiration for the American system of democracy.

Governor William Bradford

The *Bradford Manuscript* was intermittently lost and displaced for over a century and recently found after many years of diplomatic and legal maneuvering. It now reposes in the Archives Museum of the State House in Boston—a national treasure. Bradford's gripping account of the Mayflower's arrival off Cape Cod is a manuscript of 270 pages. The total list of Mayflower passengers which numbered 102, including children, saw nearly one-half dying within the first year.[17]

Bradford's writings display the clear intention of the Pilgrims:

"I must begin at the very root and rise of the same (and) I shall endeavor to manifest in plain style . . . the simple truth in all things (that we shall labor) . . . to have the right worship of God and discipline of Christ established in (their) church, according to the simplicity of the Gospel, without the mixture of men's inventions; and to have and be ruled by the laws of God's Word . . . it was most needful that the fundamental points of religion be preached in those ignorant and superstitious times . . . the more the light of the Gospel grew, the more they urged their subscriptions to these corruptions. . . . At this day the man or woman that begins to profess a religion and to serve God, must resolve himself to sustain mocks and injuries even as though he lived amongst the enemies of religion."

Bradford historically documented that those who professed and practiced Christianity would be criticized, that we should shake off the "yoke of anti-Christian bondage" and walk in the "fellowship of the Gospel, to walk in all His ways . . . and as it cost them something this ensuing history will be clear." Bradford wrote that those leaving Holland and sailing for America ". . . were set on the ways of God and they rested in His Providence to act with Christian behaviour . . ." Their pilgrimage ". . . not out of any new fangledness . . . but for sundry, weighty, and solid reasons . . . for a great hope and inward zeal . . . of laying some good foundation . . . for the propagating and advancing of the Gospel of the Kingdom of Christ . . . even as stepping stones unto others for the performance of so great a work."

Governor William Bradford, drawing upon the commonplace Puritan image of the Christian as a stranger and wayfarer gave rise to the famous name "Pilgrim fathers."

As to the word *father*, Bradford wrote:

"May not and ought not the children of these fathers rightly say: Our fathers were Englishmen who came over the great ocean, and were ready to perish in this wilderness."

Leading historians and sociologists, who have long studied the papers of Bradford and other Pilgrims who sailed with the Mayflower, made it clear that families cannot "hang together unless they have a strong core of religion . . . this means that there is a moral authority that underlies modern civilization and, if you destroy or neglect it, you put at risk an orderly society and invite chaos."

The Mayflower pilgrims had a character born of high spiritual values and lived moral lives.[18] Theirs is a story of abiding faith in God.

They knew the essential ingredients of human progress to be spiritual satisfaction and moral excellence, sharing a deep faith in God, the basic values of personal integrity and the stabilizing "family group" to be the anchor of the community.[19]

The Plymouth Founders passed the lesson to us who would follow in their footsteps that rights cannot be demanded without acceptance of responsibilities. Only then can we be truly free. This is the legacy of the Pilgrims. It is time for America to look back and find its soul.

> "Great hope and inward zeal they had of laying some good foundation . . . for propagating and advancing the Gospel of the Kingdom of Christ in these remote parts of the world, yea, though they should be put even as stepping stones unto others for the performance of so great a work."
> —**William Bradford**[20] (1590–1657)

The First Thanksgiving

In 1617, John Robinson's congregation resolved to move his church from Holland and emigrate to America. They prayed to know God's will. They knew that many would die in route because of the effects of the change of air, diet and water. They feared especially the savage Indians:

> "A cruel, barbarous and most treacherous people, whose reported practices of playing prisoners alive with shells, or cutting off

their limbs or joints and boiling them on coals in sight of the victims caused the bowels of men to grate within them."

A few crew and ten Pilgrims, which included Bradford, Winslow, and Governor Carver, landed on the beach and spent the first night on American soil. At first light they roused themselves and "prayed as usual before starting to make breakfast."[21]

The First Thanksgiving

On December 16, fourteen weeks after leaving England and five weeks after anchoring at Provincetown, the Mayflower sailed into Plymouth Harbor where shore parties began work to build a few houses. Sickness ravaged them and by 1621, half of the colonists and the ship's company died "with the living scarce able to bury the dead."

"For some strange reason, the Indians did not attack them, a fact which surprised the Pilgrim leaders. Then one day in late March, a tall, black-haired Indian carrying a bow and arrow strode boldly out of the woods and up the street towards the common house where a meeting to discuss better defense arrangements was in progress.

'Welcome!' said the Indian in English. He asked for beer. Having none at hand, they gave him some spirits, together with a meal of biscuit, butter, cheese, pudding and piece of mallard, all of which he liked well. As the Indian wore only a deerskin leather belt about his waist with a fringe about a span long or a little more, they gave him a soldier's overcoat as a present. He had

20

learnt his broken English at fishing stations in the region known now as Maine.

Within a short time Samoset (the Indian's name) returned with several other Indians with furs to trade and finally came to announce that Massatoit with sixty warriors was waiting nearby for the Pilgrim leaders to meet him. After a ceremonious greeting, the Pilgrims concluded with Massatoit a treaty of mutual assistance which assured the survival of the colony and, indeed, gave peace to Massachusetts Bay for forty years. It was an astonishing turn of events . . ."

One day Samoset had brought into the Pilgrim settlement an Indian called Tisquantum, or Squanto. He had been seized from New England in 1614 by an English sea captain, but made his escape and way home some four years later. After Massatoit returned home, Squanto stayed with the Pilgrims. He showed them how and when to plant Indian corn and where to find the best fishing places. Until his death in 1622, Squanto gave them invaluable service. Although not without some Indian faults of character, he was a true friend and guide. Bradford called him, "a special instrument sent by God for their good beyond their expectations."

The Thanksgiving in October, 1621, a festival imported from rural England, celebrated the first harvest from some 20 acres of corn fields. The 15 Pilgrims, with two new babies in their mothers' arms, entertained Massatoit and his warriors to a feast of venison, roast duck, and turkey, possibly with cranberries gathered as today in the low boggy fields where they grow in abundance.

Although they knew it not, the Pilgrims had even more cause for thanksgiving upon that autumn day for they had established the first real Puritan bridgehead in the New World. Those that followed them in the great migration of the 1630's would look upon the Pilgrims as God's pathfinders. As William Bradford reflected in his journal:

"As one candle may light a thousand, so the light here kindled has shown into many, yea, in some sort to our whole nation. Let the glorious name of Jehovah have all the praise."[22]

Not until 1863 did President Lincoln appoint the last Thursday in November as National Thanksgiving Day.

The Puritans

There has been a tendency of some historians to emphasize popular misconceptions about the uniqueness of Puritans in order to guard us against making them in our own image. This distancing of our ancestors from us can be overdone. They were not strict and dower moralists, killjoys, or even hypocrites. Instead, Puritanism covers a spectrum of beliefs from Luther and the Reformation.[23]

John Winthrop was selected governor or leader of the group because the people felt he was "sustained by a sense that God had called him."[24]

Winthrop kept a daily journal and recorded the journey and in mid-voyage delivered a lay sermon entitled "Christian Charity: A Model Hereof." He preached that it was the "spirit of Christ, the spirit of love, which would knit together a truly Christian society."[25] In order to avoid shipwreck, the passengers were to follow the "counsel of Micah," to do justly, to love mercy, to walk humbly with our God:

> "For we must consider that we shall be as a city upon a hill, the eyes of all people are upon us; so that if we shall deal falsely with our God and His work, we have undertaken and so cause Him to withdraw His present help from us, we shall be made a story and a byword through the world. Therefore, let us choose life, that we and our seed may live by obeying His voice, and cleaving to Him, for He is our life and our prosperity."

Measured by generations, the Puritan age is not all that remote from us. Puritan values and attitudes survive today, especially the Puritan ethic of work:

"The Christian must work hard in his calling in the world, for his labour is the means whereby the love of Christ in him can reach out to his neighbor."

Luther and the Puritans assumed that men were Christians . . . and the heirs of the Reformation and Renaissance tradition through education and home upbringing. This sense of vocation survives today in more-or-less secular forms.

The Puritan values of industry, thrift, sobriety, frugality, reliability, temperance, and punctuality are still there, but they serve social, material or worldly ends. Religion and economics both sanction such virtues. Failure to recognize and use one's talents is felt to be a sin against one's self and society. This restless desire to serve others by employing one's abilities to the fullest is the hallmark of the Puritan attitude towards work. Christianity is a busy trade in which laziness or idleness is unacceptable. The Puritan in modern man seeks to be constantly active. He feels an inward sense of duty—"stern daughter of the voice of God," as Wordsworth called it—which drives him to be busy. Benjamin Franklin said it best: "God helps those who help themselves."[26]

Puritanism

The main convictions of the English Puritans were carried to America by their descendants in the 1630's. They believed humankind must depend entirely upon God for salvation. They emphasized the authority of the Bible (the Bible exerts a "regulative" authority), which means Christians, so far as possible, should do only what the Scriptures explicitly direct.[27]

Puritan settlers considered themselves to be God's chosen people,[28] identifying themselves with Israel's exodus, and they believed that God had given them the Promised Land (America).[29]

Puritans believed God created society as a unified whole. Church and state, the individual and the public, are not unrelated spheres of life but are complimentary, intimately connected by God's acts of creation and His continuing providence.

At the time Puritans established Massachusetts and Virginia, according to Captain John Smith, they believed in an "honest, religious, and courageous Divine," in holding a service of communion. In 1610, when the colony teetered on the brink of collapse, their first actions were to organize a worship service to issue a biblical call for sacrifice in industry. Their earliest legal code in Virginia made attendance at Sunday services *compulsory* and contained harsh laws prohibiting violations of the Sabbath and adultery.

American Puritans were a significant early Christian experience dominating modern perceptions of America's religious past. The Puritan moral vision was so strenuous that all Americans since have been forced to react to it in some way, but it has provided the foundation for the great success of America.

Sir William Blackstone (1723–1780)

Blackstone was an English barrister whose eighteenth century treatise on the law is probably the most famous law book ever written.

Throughout the latter half of the 1700's and the first half of the 1800's, Blackstone's popularity in America was uneclipsed. His *Commentaries* were in the offices of every lawyer in the land. Candidates for the Bar routinely examined Blackstone. He was cited authoritatively in the courts and a quotation from Blackstone settled many a legal argument.[30] The founders of our nation read Blackstone with great interest.

One reason that many legal scholars today have not read the book is that Blackstone's God-centered view of law may be out of fashion in today's legal community. Blackstone was convinced that all law had its source in God. In writing about the law of nature, he penned:

> "Law of nature. This will of his *maker* is called the law of nature. For as *God*, when *he* created matter, and enured it with the principle of mobility, established certain rules . . . so, when *he* created

man, and enured with free will to conduct himself in all parts of life, *he* laid down certain immutable laws of human nature . . .

Considering the creator only a *being* of infinite power . . . and of infinite wisdom, *he* has laid down only such laws as were founded in those relations of justice, that existed in the nature of things antecedent to any positive precept. These are the eternal, immutable laws of good and evil, to which the *creator himself* and all *his dispensations* conforms . . . the law of nature, being coequal with mankind and dictated by *God himself,* is of course superior in obligation to any other. It is binding over all the globe and all countries, and all times: no human laws are of any validity if contrary to this . . ."[31]

The Minutemen

The Provincial Congress of Massachusetts, 1774, reorganized the militia, providing that over one-third of all new regiments be made up of "Minutemen." The minutemen, known as such because they would be ready to fight at a minute's notice, would drill as citizen soldiers on the parade ground, then go to the church to hear exhortation and prayer. Many times, the deacon of the church, or even the pastor, would lead the drill. They proclaimed, "Our cause is just," and believed it was their Christian duty to defend it. The Provincial Congress of Massachusetts charged the minutemen:

"You . . . are placed by Providence in the post of honor, because it is the post of danger . . . The eyes not only of North America

25

and the whole British Empire, but of all Europe, are upon you. Let us be, therefore, altogether solicitous that no disorderly behavior, nothing unbecoming our characters as Americans, *as citizens and Christians*, be justly chargeable to us."

April 15, 1775, just four days before the famous *Battle of Lexington*, was declared *A Day of Public Humiliation, Fasting, and Prayer*, by John Hancock who said:

"In circumstances dark as these, it becomes us, as Men and Christians, to reflect that, whilst every prudent Measure should be taken to ward off the impending Judgements. . . . All confidence must be withheld from the Means we use; and reposed only on that GOD who rules in the Armies of Heaven, and without whose Blessing the best human Counsels are but Foolishness—and all created Power Vanity;

It is the Happiness of his Church that, when the Powers of Earth and Hell combine against it . . . that the Throne of Grace is of the easiest access—and its Appeal thither is graciously invited by the Father of Mercies, who has assured it, that when his Children ask Bread he will not give them a Stone . . .

RESOLVED, That it be, and hereby is recommended to the good People of this Colony of all Denominations, that THURSDAY the Eleventh Day of May next be set apart as a Day of Public Humiliation, Fasting and Prayer . . . to confess the sins . . . to implore the Forgiveness of all our Transgression . . . and a blessing on the Husbandry, Manufacturers, and other lawful Employants of this People; and especially that the union of the American Colonies in Defence of their Rights (for hitherto we desire to thank Almighty GOD) may be preserved and confirmed. . . . And that AMERICA may soon behold a gracious Interposition of Heaven."

—By Order of the [Massachusetts] Provincial Congress, John Hancock, President.[32]

The Miracle at Brooklyn Heights

The Continental Army was trapped on Brooklyn Heights, sur-rounded on three sides with their backs to the East River and their reserves on Manhattan. British warships hovered at the mouth of the river, prevented from sailing and drawing the noose tight by a strong, steady northeast wind that had suddenly come up and showed no signs of abating. The American army was finished as soon as the British pressed home the attack.

For some inexplicable reason, the British stalled for one day, and though the Americans only had enough powder left to give each man two rounds, the British waited an additional morning to launch their final assault to coordinate their movement with land forces in the morning. Washington gathered every small boat that could be pressed into service and, by God's grace, there were enough men in the army from Marblehead and Salem who were expert small boat handlers because they had spent their lives on the water and knew how to move a dinghy silently through the water. The wind then died down and the flat calm enabled the boats to carry more men; the slightest sound would give their maneuver away.

Long queues of men silently formed up on the beaches and patiently waited for the boats to take off (reminiscent of Dunkirk two centuries later).

The evacuation took too long and as the shadings of pink were beginning to lighten the eastern horizon, the British could clearly see what was happening and the fleet was ready to blow the small boats out of the water.

British and American diaries recorded what happened next: A ground fog suddenly rose out of nowhere and rolled across the river blanketing everything on land and sea. Though the sun rose higher and higher, the fog remained—long after it should have been burned away. Finally with the fog shredded, the British real-ized what had happened. They ran to the shore and began firing as the last boat was just out of range. Nearly 8,000 men had been extricated from death or imprisonment and the American cause had been preserved, all without the loss of a single life.

Later, after Valley Forge and the Battles of Monmouth and Yorktown, a grateful nation unanimously insisted their General become the first President. In Washington's Inaugural Address, he gave all credit where it was due and called upon his countrymen to do the same:

> "It would be peculiarly improper to omit, in this first official act, my fervent supplication to that Almighty Being, who presides over the universe, who presides in the counsels of nations, and whose provincial aids can supply every human defect, that His benediction may consecrate to the liberties and happiness of the people of the United States . . . every step by which they have advanced to the character of an independent nation seems to have been distinguished by some token of providential agency . . . we ought to be no less persuaded that the propitious smiles of Heaven can never be expected on a nation that disregards the eternal rules of order and right, which Heaven itself has ordained."

The Federalist Papers

Alexander Hamilton (1757–1804) was the principle author of the *Federalist Papers*, though James Madison and John Jay wrote some of the essays. The works were published in newspapers throughout the Colonies which rallied grassroots support for ratification of the *Constitution*.

James Madison wrote:

"It is impossible for a man of pious reflection not to perceive in it [the Constitution] a finger of that Almighty hand which has been so frequently and signally

"Alexander Hamilton"
by John Trumbull

extended to our relief in the critical states of the revolution."

Hamilton openly confessed his faith in God and, shortly before his death at the hand of Aaron Burr, was planning to establish the "Christian Constitutional Society," an organization to preserve constitutional law and the Christian religion.[33]

First Reading of the Declaration of Independence

The *Declaration of Independence* was adopted July 4, 1776, and first read to the public at Independence Hall in Philadelphia four days later.

There was little celebration at the time. Listeners accepted the text with deep feeling and went soberly to their jobs. Five years of bitter and difficult fighting and sacrifices lay ahead before General Washington was to accept the surrender of Cornwallis at Yorktown.

John Adams wrote his wife Abigail:

"I am well aware of the toil and blood and treasure it will cost us to maintain this Declaration to support and defend these states. Yet, through all gloom, I can see the rays of ravishing light and glory."

"The Declaration of Independence"
by John Trumbull

Adams insisted July 4th should be remembered as a "Day of Deliverance by solemn acts of devotion to God Almighty."

One Nation Under God

"The second day of July, 1776, will be the most memorable epoch in the history of America, to be celebrated by succeeding generations as the great anniversary festival, commemorated as the day of deliverance by solemn acts of devotion to God Almighty from one end of the Continent to the other, from this time forward forevermore."

By 1776, ninety-eight percent of all Americans professed to be Protestant Christians. If this is a not a Christian nation, how was it originally founded?

The U.S. Supreme Court has made this pact clear throughout the centuries. In 1892, they held:

"These references add a volume of unofficial declarations to the massive organic utterances that this is a religious people . . . a Christian nation."[34]

One extremist said:

"Providence has given to our people the choice of their rulers, and it is the duty as well as the privilege and interest of our Christian nation to select and prefer Christians for our rulers."

Who was this extremist and shouldn't he apologize for his statements—as being politically incorrect? It was the Honorable John Jay, the first Chief Justice of the United States Supreme Court and author of the *Federalist Papers*.

William Gladstone, the great British statesman and prime minister, once described the American Constitution as "the most wonderful work ever struck off at a given time by the brain and purpose of man. It has withstood the most decisive of all tests, that of time, and is now the oldest written constitution in the world. The framers were men of remarkable wisdom and foresight."

By God's providence, America is a place where miracles not only happen, but where they happen all the time. The *Declaration of Independence, United States Constitution,* and *Bill of Rights* were among the first miracles.

Referring to the adoption of the *Constitution,* James Madison sent a letter to his good friend Thomas Jefferson (who was in France at the time) in October, 1787, marveling:

> "It is impossible to consider the degree of concord which ultimately prevailed as less than a miracle."[35]

In February, 1788, George Washington echoed those words when he wrote to Lafayette:

> "It appears to me, then, little short of a miracle that the delegates from so many states . . . should unite in forming a system of national government, so little liable to well founded objections."

America truly is a land of miracles. But our nation did not become this way by accident. America's famous poet, Carl Sandburg, treasured our country with the words:

> "I see America, not in the setting sun of a black night of despair ahead of us; I see America in the crimson light of a rising sun fresh from the burning, creating hand of God. I see great days ahead, great days possible to men and women of will and vision . . ."[36]
> "If she forgets where she came from, if the people lose sight of what brought them along, if she listens to the deniers and mockers, then will begin the rot and dissolution."[37]

The colonial background of the new states was overwhelmingly Protestant. It was simply that Sunday legislation, laws prohibiting atheism and promoting public morals, and the regular use of Christian language by government officials, was appropriate.

Over a century ago, President Abraham Lincoln worried about our drifting away from God:

"That this nation, under God, shall have a new birth of freedom—and that the government of the people, by the people, and for the people shall not perish from the earth."

But he saw the seeds of apostasy already plaguing our nation:

"We have been the recipients of the choicest bounties of heaven. We have been preserved, these many years, in peace and prosperity. We have grown in numbers, wealth and power, as no other nation has ever grown. But we have forgotten God. We have forgotten the gracious Hand which preserved us in peace, and multiplied and enriched and strengthened us; and we have vainly imagined, in the deceitfulness of our hearts, that all these blessings were produced by some superior wisdom and virtue of our own. Intoxicated with unbroken success, we have become too self-sufficient to feel the necessity of redeeming and preserving grace, too proud to pray to the God that made us!"[38]

Joseph Storey (1779–1845)

In 1812, Joseph Storey became the youngest judge appointed to the Supreme Court. He served a lengthy tenure (1812–1845), and was John Marshall's right hand man in defining the role of the court. Storey asserted:

"The promulgation of the great doctrines of religion . . . [can] never be a matter of indifference to any well ordered community."

He believed:

"The Christian religion, as a great basis, on which it must rest for its support and permanence."

"Christianity . . . to receive encouragement from the state, so far as was not incompatible with the private rights of conscious, and the freedom of religious worship."[39]

"In matters of religion I have considered that its free exercise is placed by the Constitution, independent of the power of the central government. I, have therefore, undertaken on no occasion to prescribe the religious exercise suited to it, but have left them, as the Constitution found them, under the direction and discipline of the church or state authorities."

Thomas Jefferson (1743–1826)

The author of the phrase "separation of church and state" was never recognized as an authority on the *First Amendment.* This recent heavy reliance on Jefferson is a new and recent phenomenon. Jefferson was rarely cited by previous courts for reasons given by Jefferson himself.

He was not part of the Constitutional Convention, and due to slow communication, any transmission of letters from him to the American convention would have required weeks. Jefferson rightly disqualified himself, and although he wanted the *Bill of Rights,* he gave vague directions concerning it:

Thomas Jefferson

"On receiving it (the Constitution while in France), I wrote strongly to Mr. Madison, urging the want of provision for the freedom of religion, freedom of the press, trial by jury, habeas corpus, the substitution of militia for a standing army, and for an expressed reservation to the States of all rights not specifically granted to the Union . . . this is all the hand I had in what related to the Constitution."

Jefferson's letter of January 1, 1802, was not a public policy paper but a private letter. If private letters are to form the basis of national policy, then it would be important to publish all of the letter and thus provide its context rather than taking only eight words from it. Joseph Storey who sat on the U.S. Supreme Court from 1811–1845 and also a professor at Harvard Law School stated:

"Probably at the time of the adoption of the Constitution, and the admendment now under consideration (First Amendment) the general if not universal sentiment in America was, that christianity ought to receive encouragement from the State so far as was not incompatible with the private rights of conscience and the freedom of religious worship. An attempt to level all religions and to make it a matter of state policy to hold all and utter indifference, would have created universal disapprobation, if not universal indignation . . ."[40]

Jefferson's Letter

"The general principles on which the fathers achieved independence were . . . the general principles of Christianity . . . I will avow that I then believed, and now believe, that these general principles of Christianity are as eternal and immutable as the existence and attributes of God."

—John Adams, *in a letter
to Thomas Jefferson,* June 28, 1813[41]

The *First Amendment* was never intended to separate Christian principles from government. The words *separation, church,* or *state* are not found in the *First Amendment* and those phrases appear in no founding documents. The congressional records of June through September, 1789, make it clear they wanted to follow God's principles, but not allow one denomination to run the nation. In 1799, the U.S. Supreme Court declared:

> "By our form of government, the Christian religion is the established religion; and all sects and denominations of Christians are placed on the same equal footing."[42]

Jefferson believed, as did other Founders, that the First Amendment simply prevented the federal establishment of a single denomination, a fact which he made clear in a letter to Benjamin Rush when he wrote he was against "the establishment of a particular form of Christianity."[43]

On November 7, 1801, the Baptists of Danbury, Connecticut, wrote Jefferson. They wondered if their religious exercise was a government-granted right rather than a God-granted right. They were worried that some day the government might try to regulate religious expression. Jefferson understood their concern. He assured them the free exercise of religion was an unalienable right which would not be meddled with by the government. He pointed out there was a "wall of separation between church and state," to ensure the government would never interfere with religious activities.[44]

To Messrs. Nehemiah Dodge and Others, a Committee of the Danbury Baptist Association, In the State of Connecticut:

"Gentlemen,

The affectionate sentiments of esteem and approbation which you are so good as to express towards me, on behalf of the Danbury Baptist Association, gives me the highest satisfaction. My duties dictate a faithful and zealous pursuit of the interests of my constituents, and in the proportion as they are persuaded of my fidelity to those duties, the discharge of them becomes more and more pleasing.

Believing with you that religion is a matter which lies solely between man and his God, that he owes account to none other for his faith or his worship, that the legislative powers of government reach actions only, and not opinions, I contemplate with sovereign reverence that act of the whole American people which declared that their legislature should "make no law respecting an establishment of religion, or prohibiting the free exercise thereof," thus building a wall of separation between church and state. Adhering to this expression of the supreme will of the nation in behalf of the rights of conscience, I shall see with sincere satisfaction the progress of those sentiments which tend to restore to man all his natural rights, convinced he has no natural right in opposition to his social duties.

I reciprocate your kind prayers for the protection and blessing of the common Father and Creator of man, and tender you for yourselves and your religious association, assurances of my high respect and esteem."

Today, all that is ever heard about Jefferson's letter is the phrase "wall of separation between church and state" without either the context or the explanation given in the letter or its application by earlier courts.

For over 150 years, the *First Amendment* was interpreted to prohibit the establishment of a single national denomination. His letter fell into disuse and remained silent until 1947 when the Court, for the first time, did not cite Jefferson's entire letter but selected eight words in Everson vs. Board of Education:

"The *First Amendment* has erected 'a wall of separation between church and state.' That wall must be kept high and impregnable."[45]

Benjamin Franklin (1706–1790)

The founding fathers were emphatic about keeping men in office who understood God's principles. In a famous speech delivered by Benjamin Franklin (1706–1790) on June 28, 1787, to the Constitutional Convention, Franklin reminded the delegates that we need God to be our friend, not our enemy; we need Him to be our ally, not our adversary; we need to make sure we have kept His "concurring aid" when he said:

"*Benjamin Franklin*" *by David Martin*

"If a sparrow cannot fall to the ground without His notice, is it probable that an empire can rise without His aid?

We've been assured in the sacred writing that, 'Except the Lord build a house, they labor in vain that build it.'"[46]

Franklin reminded the Convention that at the beginning of the war with England, the Continental Congress had prayers for divine protection. "Our prayers, Sir, were heard and they were graciously answered," as he suggested they pray before proceeding further.[47]

The myth of "the wall of separation between church and state" was not a teaching of Benjamin Franklin but has become a teaching of law only in recent years.

The *Declaration of Independence* Is Politically Incorrect

The *Declaration of Independence* might not be approved today as it is politically incorrect. It contains direct references to God, and there is no indication that any delegate objected to such references.[48]

Today, many Americans would protest the use of the word *Creator*. It would be bemoaned by liberals as the endorsement of religion by government.

On July 4, 1776, however, there was no debate over the phrase *endowed by their Creator*. That America was founded as a Christian nation is beyond debate. We were a Christian nation with a constitutional government, rather than a theocracy, but a Christian nation nonetheless. We took Judeo-Christian principles so much for granted that the Founding Fathers saw little reason to state the obvious.

"endowed by their creator"

Declaration of Independence

The *Declaration of Independence* refers to the Creator rather than to Jesus and may be an acknowledgment that not all Americans of the day believed in the latter.

There was a desire to refrain from defining America as a Christian nation because doing so would raise the question, "Whose variety of Christianity?"

George Washington (1732–1799)

George Washington as an intrepid young colonel went off to serve under Braddock in the Indian Wars in 1755. His mother sent him off with the prayer: "Remember that God only is our sure trust. To Him, I commend you. My son, neglect not the duty of secret prayer." He did not neglect it and copied prayers from the *Book of Common Prayer* into his field journal. He was regularly seen in private prayer by his men.[49]

Washington believed if anyone attempted to separate religion and morality from politics, he couldn't be called an American patriot.

Fifteen years after the Battle of Monongahela when Washington and Dr. Craik were surveying the battlefield, through an interpreter they met the Chief of the Indians who had fought against Braddock. The Chief had pointed out to his warriors the tall officer riding out in front of his concealed troops, leveled their rifles at him, and confessed:

"It was all in vain. A power mightier than we shielded him from harm. He cannot die in battle . . . listen: the Great Spirit protects that man and guides his destinies. He will become the chief of nations, and a people yet unborn will hail him as the founder of a mighty empire."

Washington proceeded to bring order out of chaos and demanded of his officers and soldiers, ". . . a punctual attendance of Divine services, to implore the blessing of Heaven

"George Washington" by Charles Willson Peale

upon the means used for our safety and defense."

When Washington, the "Father of our Country," became the first President on April 30, 1789, just as other Presidents who followed have done, he swore to uphold the office of the President of the United States. As he responded, "I swear," he took the Bible from Secretary Livingston's hands and reverently and respectfully pressed it to his lips and kissed it. Then he added, "So help me

God." Every President sworn into office since that day has repeated that prayer.

Washington was a constitutional expert—President of the convention which framed the *Constitution*, and the President of the United States who called for the formation and ratification of the *Bill of Rights* and the *First Amendment*. He understood the constitutional intent and the meaning of the *First Amendment*. He explained there are only two foundations for political prosperity in America, religion and morality, and that no one could be called an American patriot if he tried to separate those two foundations from politics:

> "Of all the dispositions and habits which lead to political prosperity, religion and morality are indispensable supports. In vain, would that man claim the tribute of Patriotism who should labour to subvert these great pillars . . ." [50]

Washington reminded Americans that they should continue to reject any tenant which asserted that one could be moral without religion. That is in the premise to the French Revolution that produced a blood bath of executions and slaughters. In America, we knew better. Washington explained:

> "Whatever may be conceded to the influence of refined education on minds, reason and experience, both prevent us to expect that national morality can prevail in exclusion of religious principles."

The phrase "separation of church and state" does not appear in the Bill of Rights or the Constitution.

Washington understood that religion was the basis of morality and self control and that morality and self control were the only firm foundations of our free government. He knew that if we lost our religious principles, we would have no secure basis for property, life, or freedom.

Washington's Farewell Address

"The Father of His Country" spent 45 years of his life in public service, from Commander-in-Chief through eight years as President, to President of the convention that gave us the *U.S. Constitution*. If anyone knew the intent of the *Constitution* and the *Bill of Rights*, it was Washington.

The Farewell Address of George Washington in 1796 has long been considered a major contribution to American political thought. Along with the *Declaration of Independence,* the *Constitution*, and the *Federalist Papers*, it is one of the greatest documents of American history.[51]

Washington wanted Americans to strengthen the better elements of their national character. He felt the connection between private and public happiness made religion and morality "a necessary spring of popular government," and an indispensable support to political prosperity.[52]

Washington warned of "the necessity of paying due attention to the moral virtues," and avoiding "the scenes of vice and dissipation." He believed that an early and proper education in manners and morals would form the leading traits of life and urged the development of the unremitting practice of moral virtue.

He knew an education needs both a "highly cultivated mind, and a proper sense of your duties to God and man."[53]

Washington hoped religious education in America would flourish and become a means by which we can receive . . . "acquiring and diffusing useful knowledge."

"I now make it my earnest prayer, that God would have you, and the State over which you preside, in his holy protection, and that he would incline the hearts of Citizens to cultivate a spirit of subordination and obedience to government . . . that he would most graciously be pleased to dispose us all, to do

Justice, to love mercy, and to demean ourselves with all that charity, humility, and pacific temper of mind, which were the Characteristics of the Divine Author of our blessed Religion an humble imitation of whose example in these things, we can never hope to be a happy Nation."[54]

"The blessed Religion revealed in the word of God will remain an eternal and awful monument to prove that the best Institutions may be abused by human depravity; and that they may even, in some instances, be made subservient to the vilest purposes."[55]

"George Washington at Princeton"
by Charles Willson Peale

Washington's Farewell Address is an aspect of our heritage which has almost totally disappeared from student texts. His Farewell Address once appeared as a separate school textbook for over a century as *the most significant political speech ever delivered to the nation.* He reminded America what had brought us to success and warned us about what must be done to continue it. He pointed *out the two foundations for political prosperity are religion and morality,* and no one could be called an American patriot who attempted to separate politics from its two foundations:

"Of all the dispositions and habits which lead to political prosperity, religion and morality are indispensable supports.

In vain would that man claim the tribute of patriotism, who should labor to subvert these great pillars."[56]

President Washington believed that if he attempted to separate religion and morality from politics, he could not be called an American patriot. We do not hear these statements of America's Founders anymore. Liberal, politically correct multiculturalists would object.

Washington believed civilized society could not endure without religion. He pondered in 1781, whether:

"the liberties of a nation be thought secure, when we have removed their only firm basis, a conviction in the minds of people that these liberties are a gift from God!"

Alexis de Tocqueville (1805–1859)

Alexis de Tocqueville was a famous French statesman, historian, and social philosopher. Beginning in 1831, he and Gustave de Beaumont toured the country of America for the purpose of observing the American people and their institutions. His two-part work which was published in 1835 and 1840, was entitled *Democracy in America*. It has been described as the most comprehensive and penetrating analysis of the relationship between character and society in America ever written. In it he related:

There is no country in the world where the Christian religion retains a greater influence over the souls of men than in America.

ALEXIS DE TOCQUEVILLE, 1831

"Upon my arrival in the United States, *the religious aspect of the country was the first thing that struck my attention; and the longer I stayed there, the more I perceived the great political consequences resulting from this new state of things.* In France I had almost always seen the spirit of religion and the spirit of freedom marching in opposite directions. But *in America I found they were immediately united and that they reigned in common over the same country. Religion in America . . . must be regarded as the foremost of the political institutions of that country;* for if it does not impart a taste for freedom, it facilitates the use of it. Indeed, it is in this same point of view that the inhabitants of the United States themselves look upon religious belief.

"The sects that exist in the United States are innumerable. They all differ in respect to the worship which is due to the Creator; but they all agree in respect to the duties which are due from man to man.

"Each sect adores the Deity in its own peculiar manner, but *all sects preach the same moral law in the name of God . . .*

"Moreover, *all the sects of the United States are comprised within the great unity of Christianity, and the Christian morality is everywhere the same.*

"In the United States *the sovereign authority is religious, . . . there is no country in the world where the Christian religion retains a greater influence over the souls of men than in America,* and there can be no greater proof of its utility and of its conformity to human nature than that its influence is powerfully felt over the most enlightened and free nation of the earth.

"In the United States, if a political character attacks a sect [denomination], this may not prevent even the partisans of that very sect, from supporting him; but if he attacks all the sects together [Christianity], every one abandons him and he remains alone.

"I do not question that the great austerity of manners that is observable in the United States arises, in the first instance, from religious faith . . . its influence over the mind of woman is supreme, and women are the protectors of morals. There is certainly no country in the world where the tie of marriage is more respected than in America or where conjugal happiness is more highly or worthily appreciated . . .

"Christianity, therefore reigns without obstacle, by universal consent; the consequence is, as I have before observed, that every principle of the moral world is fixed and determinate . . .

"Not until I went into the churches of America and heard her pulpits flame with righteousness did I understand the secret of her genius and power."

"America is great because America is good, and if America ever ceases to be good, America will cease to be great."

The principles of genuine liberty, and of wise laws and administrations, are to be drawn from the Bible and sustained by its authority.

"The Americans combine the notions of Christianity and of liberty so intimately in their minds, that it is impossible to make them conceive the one without the other."
"Christianity is the companion of liberty in all its conflicts— the cradle of its infancy, and the divine source of its claims."

"They brought with them . . . a form of Christianity, which I cannot better describe, than by styling it a democratic and republican religion. . . . From the earliest settlement of the emigrants, politics, and religion contracted an alliance which has never been dissolved."

In August of 1831, while traveling through Chester County in New York, Alexis de Tocqueville had the opportunity to observe a court case. He wrote:

"While I was in America, a witness, who happened to be called at the assizes of the county of Chester (state of New York), declared that he did not believe in the existence of God or in the immortality of the soul. The judge refused to admit his evidence, on the ground that the witness had destroyed beforehand all confidence of the court in what he was about to say. The newspapers related the fact without any further comment. *The New York Spectator* of August 23rd, 1831, relates the fact in the following terms:

'The court of common pleas of Chester County (New York,) a few days since rejected a witness who declared his disbelief in the existence of God. The presiding judge remarked, that he had not before been aware that there was a man living who did not believe in the existence of God; that this belief constituted the sanction of all testimony in a court of justice: and that he knew of no case in a Christian country, where a witness had been permitted to testify without such a belief.'"[57]

McGuffey's Reader

William Holmes McGuffey (1800–1873), an American educator, was the president of Ohio University and professor at the University of Virginia and University of Ohio. Considered the "Schoolmaster of the Nation," McGuffey published *McGuffey's Reader* in 1836. This book was the mainstay in public education in

19th Century Schoolhouse

America until 1920. As of 1863, 125 million copies had been sold, making it the most widely used and influential textbook of all times.

Millions of American children learned to read and write from that reader. In its forward, McGuffey wrote:

> "The Christian religion is the religion of our country. From it are derived our prevalent notions of the character of God, the great moral governor of the universe. On its doctrines are founded the peculiarities of our free institutions."

> "The Ten Commandments and the teachings of Jesus are not only basic but plenary."

Lesson 37 of McGuffey's *Eclectic First Reader* is entitled "Evening Prayer":

> "At the close of the day, before you go to sleep, you should not fail to pray to God to keep you from sin and from harm. You ask your friends for food, and drink, and books, and clothes; and when they give you these things, you thank them, and love them for the good they do you. You should ask your God for these things which he can give you, and which no one else can give you.
>
> You should ask him for life, and health, and strength; and you should pray to him to keep your feet from the ways of sin and shame. You should thank him for all his good gifts; and learn, while young, to put your trust in him; and the kind care of God will be with you, both in your youth and in your old age."

In his preface to his 1836 *Eclectic Third Reader*, McGuffey states:

> "In making [my] selections, [I have] drawn from the purest foundations of English literature. . . . For the copious extracts made from the Sacred Scripture, [I make] no apology.
>
> Indeed, upon a review of the work, [I am] not sure but an apology may be due for [my] not having still more liberally transferred to [my] pages the chaste simplicity, the thrilling pathos, the living descriptions, and the matchless sublimity of the sacred writings.

From no source has the author drawn more copiously than from the Sacred Scriptures. For this [I] certainly apprehend no censure. In a Christian country, that man is to be pitied, who, at this day, can honestly object to imbuing the minds of youth with the language and spirit of the Word of God."

In his 1837 *Eclectic Third Reader*, McGuffey instructs:

"1. The design of the Bible is evidently to give us correct information concerning the creation of all things, by the omnipotent Word of God; to make known to us the state of holiness and happiness of our first parents in paradise, and their dreadful fall from that condition by transgression against God, which is the original cause of all our sin and misery . . .

3. The Scriptures are especially designed to make us wise unto salvation through faith in Christ Jesus; to reveal to us the mercy of the Lord in him; to form our minds after the likeness of God our Saviour, to build up our souls in wisdom and faith, in love and holiness; to make us thoroughly furnished unto good works, enabling us to glorify God on earth; and, to lead us to an imperishable inheritance among the spirits of just men made perfect, and finally to be glorified with Christ in heaven."

McGuffey's Reader educated millions of our nation's youth. Today, however, it would be politically incorrect.

Noah Webster (1758–1843)

"God's Word, contained in the Bible, has furnished all necessary rules to direct our conduct."[58]

In 1832, Noah Webster published his *History of The United States*, in which he wrote:

"The brief exposition of the Constitution of the United States, will unfold to young persons the principles of republican government; and it is the sincere desire of the writer that our citizens should early understand that the genuine source of correct republican principles is the Bible, particularly the New Testament or the Christian religion . . .

The moral principles and precepts contained in the Scriptures ought to form the basis of all of our civil constitutions and laws. . . . All the miseries and evils which men suffer from vice, crime, ambition, injustice, oppression, slavery and war, proceed from their despising or neglecting the precepts contained in the Bible.

When you become entitled to exercise the right of voting for public officers, let it be impressed on your mind that God commands you to choose for rulers just men who will rule in the fear of God . . .

If the citizens neglect their duty and place unprincipled men in office, the government will soon be corrupted; laws will be made not for the public good so much as for the selfish or local purposes;

Corrupt or incompetent men will be appointed to execute the laws; the public revenues will be squandered on unworthy men; and the rights of citizens will be violated or disregarded.

If a republican government fails to secure public prosperity and happiness, it must be because the citizens neglect the Divine commands, and elect bad men to make and administer the laws."

In 1832, Webster published *Advice to the Young*, in which he stated:

The 'Advice to the Young' . . . will be useful in enlightening the minds of youth in religious and moral principles, and serve . . . to restrain some of the common vices of our country. . . . To exterminate our popular vices is a work of far more importance to the character and happiness of our citizens than any other improvements in our system of education."

In 1833, Webster translated the *Common Version of the Holy Bible, Containing the Old and New Testament, with Amendments of the Language*. In the preface he wrote:

The Bible is the Chief moral cause of all that is good, and the best corrector of all that is evil, in human society; the best book for regulating the temporal concerns of men, and the only book that can serve as an infallible guide to future felicity . . . It is extremely important to our nation, in a political as well as religious view, that all possible authority and influence should be given to the scriptures, for these furnish the best principles of civil liberty, and the most effectual support of republican government.

The principles of genuine liberty, and of wise laws and administrations, are to be drawn from the Bible and sustained by its authority. The man, therefore, who weakens or destroys the divine authority of that Book may be accessory to all the public disorders which society is doomed to suffer . . .

There are two powers only, sufficient to control men and secure the rights of individuals and a peaceable administration; these are the combined force of religion and law, and the force or fear of the bayonet."[59]

Last Wills and Testaments

Much has been said about what our founding fathers believed. But it is important, regardless of what they spoke or wrote during their lifetimes, to see what they believed *at the end of their lives.* Their own declarations in their *Last Wills and Testaments* disprove assertions that our Founding Fathers were deists or Unitarians, believing in some form of impersonal Providence but rejecting the divinity of Jesus and the relevance of the Bible.

These Wills may be obtained through historical societies, but the assertions contained in their Wills speak loud and clear that the great majority of our Founding Fathers were believers in Jesus Christ. For example:

"I am a real Christian, that is to say, a disciple of the doctrines of Jesus Christ."

—Thomas Jefferson (1826)

"You do well to learn . . . above all the religion of Jesus Christ."
—George Washington (1799)

"To my Creator I resign myself humbly confiding in His goodness and in His mercy through Jesus Christ for the events of eternity."

—**John Dickinson,**
Signer of the Constitution (1732–1808)

"First of all, I . . . rely upon the merits of Jesus Christ for a pardon of all my sins."

—**Samuel Adams,**
Signer of the Declaration (1722–1803)

"I have a tender reliance on the mercy of the Almighty; through the merits of the Lord Jesus Christ. I am a sinner. I look to Him for mercy. Pray for me."

—**Alexander Hamilton (1755–1804)**

"I resign my soul into the hands of the Almighty who gave it in humble hopes of his mercy through our Savior Jesus Christ."

—**Gabriel Duvall, (1844),**
***U.S. Supreme Court Justice selected
as a delegate to the Constitutional Convention***

"This is all the inheritance I can give to my dear family. The religion of Christ can give them one which will make them rich indeed."

—**Patrick Henry (1736–1799)**

"I render sincere and humble thanks for His manifold and unmerited blessings, and especially for our redemption and salvation by his beloved Son . . . Blessed be his holy name."

—**John Jay, (1745–1829)**
***First Chief Justice
U.S. Supreme Court***

"John Jay"
by Trumbull

"I am constrained to express my adoration of . . . the Author of my existence . . . [for] His forgiving mercy revealed to the world through Jesus Christ, through whom I hope for never ending happiness in a future state."

—**Robert Treat Paine, (1731–1814)**
Signer of the Declaration

"I think it proper here not only to subscribe to . . . doctrines of the Christian religion . . . but also, in the bowels of a father's affection, to exhort and charge them [my children] that the fear of God is the beginning of wisdom, that the way of life held up in the Christian system is calculated for the most complete happiness."
—Richard Stockton, (1730–1781)
Signer of the Declaration

Personal Writings

The *personal writings* of numerous other Founders contain equally strong declarations.

"My hopes of a future life are all founded upon the Gospel of Christ and I cannot cavil or quibble away [evade or object to] . . . the whole tenor of His conduct by which He sometimes positively asserted and at others countenances [permits] His disciples in asserting that He was God."
—John Quincy Adams (1767–1848)
Sixth President of the United States,
1825–1829

"Now to the triune God, The Father, the Son, and the Holy Ghost, be ascribed all honor and dominion forevermore-Amen."
—Gunning Bedford, Jr. (1747–1812)
Signer of the Constitution

"You have been instructed from your childhood in the knowledge of your lost state by nature the absolute necessity of a change of heart, and an entire renovation of soul to the image of Jesus Christ—of salvation thro' His meritorious righteousness only— and the indispensable necessity of personal holiness without which no man shall see the Lord."
—Elias Boudinot, (1740–1821)
Revolutionary Officer and President of the
Continental Congress (to his daughter)

"Don't forget to be a Christian. I have said much to you on this day and I hope an indelible impression is made."
—Jacob Broom, (1752–1810) *Signer of the Constitution (to his son)*

"On the mercy of my Redeemer I rely for salvation and on His merits, not on the works I have done in obedience to His precepts."
—Charles Carroll, (1737–1832) *Signer of the Declaration*

"I think the Christian religion is a Divine institution; and I pray to God that I may never forget the precepts of His religion or suffer the appearance of an inconsistency in my principles and practice."
—James Iredell, (1799) *U.S. Supreme Court Justice under President George Washington*

"My only hope of salvation is in the infinite, transcendent love of God manifested to the world by the death of His Son upon the Cross. Nothing but His blood will wash away my sins. I rely exclusively upon it. Come, Lord Jesus! Come quickly!"
—Benjamin Rush, (1739–1800) *Signer of the Declaration*

"I believe that there is one only living and true God, existing in three persons, the Father, the Son, and the Holy Ghost, the same in substance, equal in power and glory. That the Scriptures of the old and new testaments are a revelation from God and a complete rule to direct us how we may glorify and enjoy Him."
—Roger Sherman, (1721–1793) *Signer of both the Declaration and the Constitution*

"I shall now entreat . . . you in the most earnest manner to believe in Jesus Christ, for 'there is no salvation in any other' [Acts 4:12] . . . [I]f you are not clothed with the spotless robe of His righteousness, you must forever perish."
—John Witherspoon, (1723–1794) *Signer of the Declaration*

"Indeed, I tremble for my country when I reflect that God is just; that his justice cannot sleep forever."

—Thomas Jefferson, 1794

The Source of Our Laws

Our Founding Fathers delivered to us a system of government that has enjoyed unprecedented success. We are the world's longest ongoing constitutional republic. More than two hundred years under the same document, and under one form of government is an accomplishment unknown among contemporary nations.

Where did our founding fathers acquire the ideas that produced such longevity? From what sources did our founders choose their ideas?

Political science professors at the University of Houston recently collected all writings from the founding era to see whom the Founders were quoting. Researchers assembled over 15,000 writings (no small sample) and searched those writings.

The project spanned 10 years but by the end of their work, the researchers isolated 3,154 direct quotes made by the Founders and identified the source of those quotes.

The man most quoted by the founding fathers (8.3 percent) was Baron Charles de Montesquieiu. Sir William Blackstone was second (7.9 percent), and John Locke was third (2.9 percent).

Surprisingly, researchers discovered that the Founders quoted directly out of the Bible four times more often than they quoted Montesquieiu, four times more than Blackstone, and twelve times more than John Locke. Thirty-four percent (34%) of all the Founding Fathers' quotes came directly out of the Bible.

The study was even more impressive when the source of the ideas used were identified. Blackstone was concerned with the laws since he wrote one of the most famous law books ever written, *Blackstone's Commentaries on the Laws* (1768). Lawyers for over one century quoted Blackstone to settle disputes, define words, and examine procedures. Amazingly, many of the quotes taken from Blackstone prove that he used the Bible to arrive at his conclusions.

The concept for three branches of government, for instance, can be found in Isaiah 33:22, the logic for the separation of powers is based on Jeremiah 17:9, the basis of tax exemptions of churches is found in Ezra 7:24, and there are many other examples.

Biblical heritage was so well understood during the early years of our nation, the U.S. Supreme Court declared in 1892:

> "No purpose of action against religion can be imputed to any legislation, state or national, because this is a religious people . . . this is a Christian nation."[60]

The U.S. Supreme Court provided 87 different historical precedents to support its conclusions, quoting the founding fathers, their action, congressional acts, and legislation form of state government, all which concluded we were a Christian nation.

Since courts base their decision on precedents, you can go back and study the 87 precedents quoted by the Court sufficient to conclude that we were a Christian nation. In 1844, when a Philadelphia school announced that it would teach morality but no longer teach religion, our highest Court said:

> "Why may not the Bible, and especially the New Testament . . . be read and taught as a divine revelation in the (school), its general precepts expounded . . . and its glorious principles of morality incalculated? . . . where can the purest principles of morality be learned so clearly or so perfectly as from the New Testament?"[61]

In 1811, the U.S. Supreme Court ruled:

"Whoever strikes at the root of Christianity tends manifestly to the dissolution of civil government."[62]

The court said that an attack on Jesus Christ was an attack on Christianity; an attack on Christianity was an attack on the foundation of this country; therefore, *an attack on Jesus Christ was equivalent to an attack on our country*!

United States Presidents

"It is impossible rightly to govern the world without God and the Bible."

—George Washington

"Let me live according to those holy rules which Thou hast this day prescribed in Thy Holy Word . . . Direct me to the true object, Jesus Christ the way, the truth, and the life. Bless, O Lord, all the people of this land."

—George Washington, 1752[63]

"Suppose a nation in some distant region should take the Bible for their only Law Book, and every member should regulate his conduct by the precepts there exhibited. . . . What a paradise would this region be!"

—John Adams, (1735–1826)

"The Bible is the rock on which our republic rests."

—Andrew Jackson (1767–1845)

"Why is that, next to the birthday of the Savior of the world, your most joyous and most venerated festival returns on July 4th?

. . . it is not that, in the chain of human events, the birthday of the nation is indissolubly linked with the birthday of the Savior? That it forms a leading event in the progress of the Gospel dispensation? It is not that the Declaration of Independence first organized the social compact of the foundation of the Redeemer's mission upon earth? That it laid the cornerstone of human government upon the first precepts of Christianity?

—John Quincy Adams,
July 4, 1837

"The foundations of our society and our government rest so much on the Teachings of the Bible that it would be difficult to support them if faith in these teachings would cease to be practically universal in our country."

—Calvin Coolidge, (1872–1933)

The Santa Maria, Pinta, and the Nina set sail August 3, 1492, and by October 12th (now proclaimed Columbus Day), when the cry, "Land ho!" sounded from the crow's nest crew, they set foot on a sandy island and called it San Salvador (which means "Holy Savior") ". . . in honor of the Savior who safely brought us here," said Columbus.

The cross at the landing place, San Salvador

"Embarkation of Pilgrims" by Robert Weir

This painting hangs in the Rotunda with seven other historical paintings. The artist shows the group praying as they set out from Holland in 1620 for England and the New World.

Puritans going to worship

"Mayflower Compact" by Percy Moran

The first document in the New World to assure government by the rule of the majority was the Mayflower Compact, signed aboard ship off the coast of Cape Cod. Percy Moran painted this incident as it may have occurred.

Mayflower Compact

November 11, 1620

In the name of God Amen. We whose names are underwritten, the Loyal subjects of our dread Soveraigne Lord King James, by the grace of God, of great Britaine, Franc, & Ireland King, defender of the faith, &c. Having undertaken, for the glorie of God, and advancement of the christian faith and honour of our king & countrie, a voyage to plant the first colonie in the Northerne parts of Virginia. Do by these presents solemnly and mutualy in the presence of God, and one of another, covenant, & combine our-selves togeather into a civill body politick; for our better ordering, & preservation & furtherance of the ends aforesaid; and by vertue hearof to enacte, constitute, and frame such just & equall Lawes, ordinances, Acts, consitutions, & offices, from time to time, as shall be thought most meete & convenient for the generall good of the colonie: unto which we promise all due submission and obedience. In witness wherof we have hereunder subscribed our names at Cape Codd the 11 of November, in the year of the raigne of our soveraigne Lord King James of England, France, & Ireland the eighteenth, and of Scotland the fiftie fourth. Ano: Dom. 1620.

John Carver	*William Bradford*	*Edward Winslow*	
William Brewster	*Miles Standish*	*John Alden*	
John Billington	*Joses Fletcher*	*Isaac Allerton*	*John Turner*
Francis Eaton	*James Chilton*	*John Cranton*	*John Goodman*
Samuel Fuller	*Christopher Martin*	*William Mullins*	
William White	*Richard Warren*	*John Howland*	
Stephen Hopkins	*Digery Priest*	*Thomas Williams*	
Gilbert Winslow	*Edmund Margesson*	*Peter Brown*	
Richard Butteridge	*George Soule*	*Edward Tilly*	*John Tilly*
Francis Cooke	*Thomas Rogers*	*Thomas Tinker*	
John Ridgate	*Edward Fuller*	*Richard Clark*	
Richard Gardiner	*John Allerton*	*Thomas English*	
Edward Doten	*Edward Liester*		

"In the name of God, Amen . . . for the glorie of God, and advancement of the Christian faith . . .

Christopher Columbus erecting the cross

Westward Takes Way

Treaty with Indians

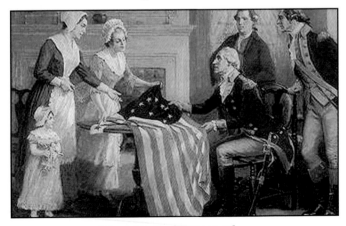

First United States Flag

"Baptism of Pocahontas" by John G. Chapman

This painting hangs in the Main Rotunda of the United States Capitol

Marriage of Washington

Washington Sworn into Office

Oath-Taking Ceremony

The conduct of the Framers . . . makes it abundantly clear that they never intended the Establishment Clause to forbid the government from publicly acknowledging our nation's religious heritage.

Washington at Valley Forge

The brutal winter of 1777 offered little hope for the Continental Army. With barely a scrap to eat, clothed in tattered rags, the soldiers endured days of frigid temperatures at Valley Forge, Pennsylvania. Some doubted whether these brave men would survive the cold months – much less be ready for battle.

While British soldiers were warm and well-fed in Philadelphia, General George Washington stayed with his starving, freezing army.

Legend has it that Washington prayed to God for strength and intervention on behalf of his men. After he wrote the governor of New Jersey and was turned down for food and clothing, where else could he turn but to God?

Washington said that he chose to call on "that all wise and powerful Being on whom alone our success depends." If our first President realized the necessity of the Lord's sovereign intervention, shouldn't we follow his example?

Prayer at Valley Forge

Washington Crossing the Delaware River

The Spirit of the '76

Washington in Courthouse

Peace Table - Yorktown

In the beginning of the contest with Great Britain, when we were sensible of danger, we had daily prayers in this room for divine protection. Our prayers were heard, and they were graciously answered . . . Have we now forgotten this powerful friend? or do we no longer need his assistance?

I have lived a long time, Sir, and the longer I live, the more convincing proofs I see of this truth: "that God governs the affairs of man." And if a sparrow cannot fall to the ground without his notice, is it probable that an empire can rise without His aid?

—Benjamin Franklin to
the Constitutional Congress
June 28, 1787

"In matters of religion, I have considered that its free exercise is placed by the Constitution independent of the powers of the General Government. I have therefore undertaken, on no occasion, to prescribe the religious exercise suited to it; but have left them, as the Constitution found them, under the direction and discipline of the state and church authorities."

—Thomas Jefferson

"*Whereas it is the duty of all nations to acknowledge the providence of the Almighty God, to obey his will, to be grateful for His benefits, and humbly implore his protection and favor . . .*"

—George Washington

"*The first and almost the only book deserving of universal attention is the Bible.*"

—John Quincy Adams

"All the good from the Saviour of the world is communicated through this Book; but for the Book we could not know right from wrong. All the things desirable to man are contained in it."

—Abraham Lincoln

"... the Bible ... is the one supreme source of revelation of the meaning of life, the nature of God and spiritual nature and need of men. It is the only guide of life which

really leads the spirit in the way of peace and salvation."

—Woodrow Wilson

"We have been the recipients of the choicest bounties of heaven. We have been preserved, these many years, in peace and prosperity. We have grown in numbers, wealth and power, as no other nation has ever grown. But we have forgotten God. We have forgotten the gracious hand which preserved us in peace, and multiplied and enriched and strengthened us; and we have vainly imagined, in the deceitfulness of our hearts, that all these blessings were produced by some superior wisdom and virtue of our own. Intoxicated with unbroken success, we have become too self-sufficient to feel the necessity of redeeming and preserving grace, too proud to pray to the God that made us! It behooves us, then to humble ourselves before the offended power, to confess our national sins, and to pray for clemency and forgiveness."

—April 30, 1863
President Abraham
Lincoln's Proclamation for a National
Day of Fasting, Humiliation
and Prayer

"Go to the Scriptures . . . the joyful promise it contains will be a balsam to all your troubles.
—Andrew Jackson

"The foundations of our society and our government rest so much on the teachings of the Bible that it would be difficult to support them in faith if these teachings would cease to be practically universal in our country."

—Calvin Coolidge

". . . And that government of the people, by the people, and for the people shall not perish from the earth."

—*Abraham Lincoln*

"Proclaim liberty through all the land and to all the inhabitants thereof."

The Liberty Bell was cast in August, 1752, in England. The inscription cast onto the Liberty Bell is an excerpt from Leviticus 25:10:

"And ye shall make hollow the fiftieth year, and proclaim liberty throughout all the land unto all the inhabitants thereof; it shall be a jubilee."

The Fundamental Orders of Connecticut (1639)

"For as much as it hath pleased Almighty God by the wise disposition of his divine providence so to order and dispose of things . . . and well knowing where a people are gathered together the word of God requires that to maintain the peace and union of such a people that there should be orderly and decent Government established according to God . . . and do for ourselves and our successors and such as shall be adjoined to us at any time hereafter, enter into Combination and Confederation together, to maintain and preserve the liberty and purity of the Gospel of our Lord Jesus which we now profess, as also, the discipline of the Churches, which according to the truth of the said Gospel is now practiced amongst us . . ."

The First Amendment

"Congress shall make no law respecting an establishment of religion, or prohibiting the free exercise thereof; or abridging the freedom of speech, or of the press; or the right of the people peaceably to assemble, and to petition the Government for redress of grievances."

This plaque is in the Everett Dirksen Office Building, Washington, D.C.

The Articles of Confederation

The Articles of Confederation, adopted by Congress in 1777 and ratified in 1781, served as the nation's fundamental law before the *Constitution*. The Articles referred to the "Great Governor of the World," and provided the model for federal non-interference in state religious affairs,[1] but the document did not delegate any authority in religious matters to the federal government.[2]

1. Articles of Confederation of 1781, Article XIII.
2. Adams, Arlin M. and Emerich, Charles J., A Nation Dedicated to Religious Liberty. (Philadelphia: University of Pennsylvania Press, 1990), p. 10.

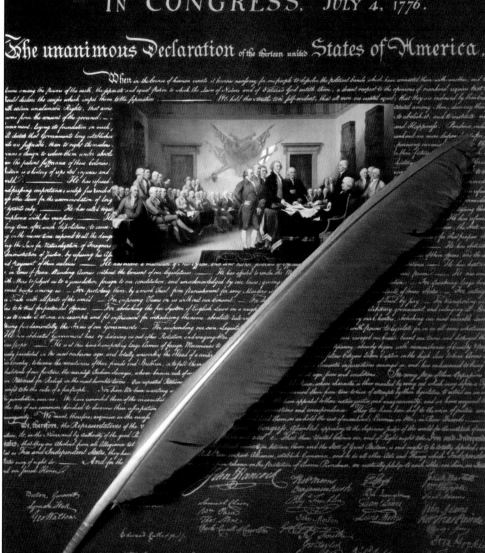

The Declaration of Independence was signed July 2, 1776, and approved by the Continental Congress. On July 4, 1776, the delegates voted to accept it and declared America's Independence from Great Britain. On July 8th, it was read in the public for the first time outside Independence Hall, Philadelphia, Pennsylvania, accompanied by the ringing of the Liberty Bell.

First Prayer in Congress

From the official journals of the Continental Congress: September 6, 1774 re-solved: That the Rev. Mr. Duché be desired to open the Congress tomorrow morning with prayers. September 6, 1774 Voted: That the thanks of the Congress be given to the Rev. Duché . . . for performing divine service, and for the excellent prayer which he composed and delivered on the occasion.

Cesar Rodney, Del.	10. - Peyton Randolph, Va.	19. - John Dehart, N.J.	28. - Samuel Chase, M.D.
Edward Rutledge, S.C.	11. - Col. N. Folsom, N.H.	20. - William Livingston, N.J.	29. - John Morton, Pa.
T. Cushing, Mass.	12. - Robert Treat Paine, Mass.	21. - Thomas McKean, Del.	30. - Thomas Mifflin, Pa.
Ephilet Dyer, Conn.	13. - George Read, Del.	22. - Roger Sherman, Conn.	31. - Charles Thompson, Va.
Samuel Adams, Mass.	14. - Silas Dean, Conn.	23. - William Paca, M.D.	32. - Rich. Henrey Lee, Va.
John Adams, Mass.	15. - Richard Smith, N.J.	24. - Rev. Mr. Duché, Pa.	33. - John Jay, N.Y.
Patrick Henry, Va.	16. - Philip Livingston, N.Y.	25. - Samuel Rhodes, Pa.	34. - Isaac Low, N.Y.
John Rutledge, S.C.	17. - Thomas Lynch, S.C.	26. - Col. William Floyd, N.Y.	35. - Benjamin Harrison, Va.
George Washington, Va.	18. - Stephen Hopkins, R.I.	27. - Stephen Crane, N.J.	36. - Samuel Ward, R.I.

"Justice Lifts the Nations" by Paul Robert (1604)

Note the sword pointing to the open scripture and Bible for guidance with no blindfold. In the 1860s, a French cartoonist, making fun of a judge with whom he disagreed, drew a cartoon of *Justice Lifts the Nations* in which he removed the sword pointing to the Bible and instead drew a blindfold.

Ironically, the cartoon has been America's symbol for law and justice since that time.

Moses with the Ten Commandments–
(Sculpture in the
Supreme Court Building)

"God who gave us life gave us liberty. Can the liberties of a nation be secure when we have removed a conviction that these liberties are the gift of God? Indeed I tremble for my country when I reflect that God is just, that his justice cannot sleep forever."
—Thomas Jefferson

According to Jefferson and the Court, the government could interfere with religion only when its actions were "subversive of good order" or "broke out into overt acts against peace and good order."

Prayer and Bible study groups are a common feature of Capitol Hill life. A small private room in the Capitol Building serves as a place of prayer and meditation for Senators and Congressman. A picture of George Washington praying serves as a focal point. In capital letters appear the inscription: "This nation under God."

"Our laws and our institutions must necessarily be based upon and embody the teachings of The Redeemer of mankind. It is impossible that it should be otherwise; and in this sense and to this extent our civilization and our institutions are emphatically Christian. . . . This is a religious people. This is historically true. From the discovery of this continent to the present hour, there is a single voice making this affirmation . . . we find everywhere a clear recognition of the same truth. . . . These, and many other matters which might be noticed, add a volume of unofficial declarations to the mass of organic utterances that this is a Christian nation."

—U.S. Supreme Court, (1892)
Church of the Holy Trinity vs. United
States

Every coin minted in the United States bears the words, "**Liberty-In God We Trust**." It was not an accident that our Forefathers chose these inseparable words, but in gratitude, to acknowledge that God has made and preserved our nation. They were confident that God's blessing was upon their endeavors because they acknowledged Him and sought His aid in all their doing. They warned future generations that the day God was not earnestly revered in America, she would become a byword among nations.

The Great Seal of the United States contains a pyramid with an eye and a triangle at the top of the pyramid with the words "Annit Coeptis" which means "**God has favored our undertakings.**"

"Here rests in honored glory an American soldier **known only to God**." The Tomb of the Unknown Soldier, the sacred burial place of an unknown soldier, is designated in a 72-ton block of white marble. The permanent marching and changing of the honor guard demonstrates duty to God and country, performed with pride and dignity.

The Supreme Court building opened in 1935. Its marble bas-relief work inside and outside portray such themes as *The Ten Commandments* above the Chief Justice's head, *Justice, the Guardian of Liberty*, and Moses holding the two tables of the Law in the center.

In 1954, Congress created a "prayer room" in the Nation's Capitol on the west side of the Rotunda. It contains an altar and an open Bible, and its stained glass window pictures George Washington in prayer along with the words of Psalm 16:1, **"Keep me safe, O God, for in you I take refuge."**

Each day of business, Congress begins with prayers led by the Senate Chaplain and House Chaplain. These prayers are also printed in the Congressional Record, a written account of each day's business.

Our national motto, **"In God We Trust"** is, by law, placed on our money and engraved on the walls of both the House and Senate Chambers.

The Washington Monument is over 550 feet tall, and at its top is a metal cap that reads, **"Praise be to God."**

"I pledge allegiance to the flag of the United States of America, and to the Republic for which it stands, **one Nation under God** indivisible with liberty and justice for all."

"Can the liberties of a nation be secure when we removed a conviction that these liberties are the gift of God?"

—Thomas Jefferson

Pearl Harbor Memorial

Viet Nam War Memorial

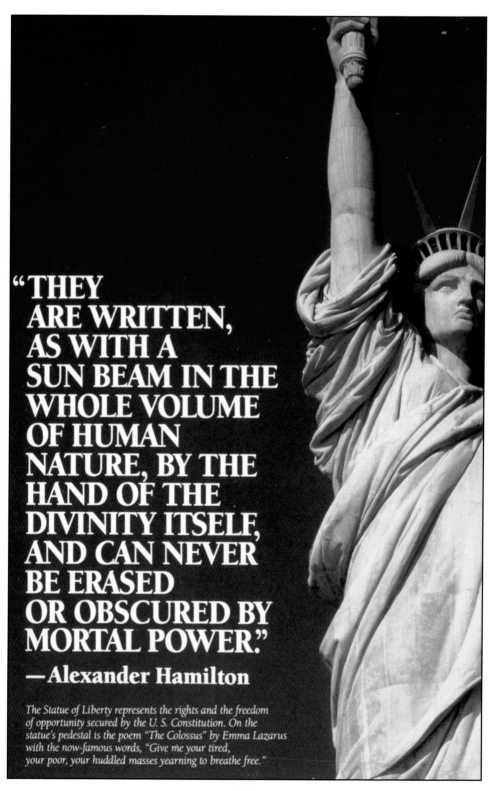

"THEY ARE WRITTEN, AS WITH A SUN BEAM IN THE WHOLE VOLUME OF HUMAN NATURE, BY THE HAND OF THE DIVINITY ITSELF, AND CAN NEVER BE ERASED OR OBSCURED BY MORTAL POWER."

—Alexander Hamilton

The Statue of Liberty represents the rights and the freedom of opportunity secured by the U. S. Constitution. On the statue's pedestal is the poem "The Colossus" by Emma Lazarus with the now-famous words, "Give me your tired, your poor, your huddled masses yearning to breathe free."

George Washington, Proclamation:
A National Thanksgiving, 1789[1]

Whereas it is the duty of all nations to acknowledge the providence of Almighty God, to obey His will, to be grateful for His benefits, and humbly to implore His protection and favor; and

Whereas both Houses of Congress have, by their joint committee, requested me "to recommend to the people of the United States a day of public thanksgiving and prayer, to be observed by acknowledging with grateful hearts the many and signal favors of Almighty God, especially by affording them an opportunity peaceably to establish a form of government for their safety and happiness."

Now, therefore, I do recommend and assign Thursday, the 26th day of November next, to be devoted by the people of these States to the services of that great and glorious Being who is the beneficent author of all the good that was, that is, or that will be; that we may then all united in rendering unto Him our sincere and humble thanks for His kind care and protection of the people and this country previous to their becoming a nation; for the signal and manifold mercies and the favorable interpositions of His providence in the course and conclusion of the late war; for the great degree of tranquility, union, and plenty in which we have since enjoyed; for the peaceable and rational manner in which we have been enabled to establish constitutions of government for our safety and happiness, and particularly the national one now lately instituted; for the civil and religious liberty with which we are blessed, and the means we have of acquiring and diffusing useful knowledge; and, in general, for all the great and various favors which He has been pleased to confer upon us.

And also that we may then unite in most humbly offering our prayers and supplications to the great Lord and Ruler of Nations, and beseech Him to pardon our national and other transgressions; to enable us all, whether in public or private stations, to perform our several and relative duties properly and punctually; to render our National Government a blessing to all the people by constantly being a Governor of wise, just, and constitutional laws, discreetly and faithfully executed and obeyed; to protect and guide all sovereigns and nations (especially such as have shown kindness to us), and to bless them with good governments, peace, and concord; to promote the knowledge and practice of true religion and virtue, and the increase of science among them and us; and, generally, to grant unto all mankind such a degree of temporal prosperity as He alone knows to be best.

Given under my hand, at the city of New York, the 3rd day of October, A.D. 1789.

---

1. Washington, Proclamation: A National Thanksgiving (October 3, 1789), in I.J. Richardson, *A Compilation of the Messages and Papers of the Presidents 1789–1908)*, at 64 (1908).

I am much afraid that schools will prove to be great gates of hell unless they diligently labor in explaining the Holy Scriptures, engraving them in the hearts of youths. I advise no one to place his child where the Scripture does not reign paramount. Every institution in which men are not increasingly occupied with the Word of God must become corrupt.

—Martin Luther

Pledge of Allegiance

I pledge allegiance to the flag of the United States of America and to the Republic for which it stands, **one Nation under God** *indivisible with liberty and justice for all.*

The Battle Hymn of the Republic

Words: Julia Ward Howe
Music: American Folk Song, 19th Century

Mine eyes have seen the glory of the coming of the Lord;
He is trampling out the vintage where the grapes of wrath
are stored;

He hath loosed the fateful lightning of His terrible swift sword;
His truth is marching on.

I have seen Him in the watchfires of a hundred circling camps;
They have builded Him an altar in the evening dews and damps;
I can read His righteous sentence by the dim and flaring lamps;
His day is marching on.

He has sounded forth the trumpet that shall never call retreat;
He is sifting out the hearts of men before His judgment seat;
O be swift, my soul, to answer Him; be jubilant, my feet!
Our God is marching on.

In the beauty of the lilies, Christ was born across the sea;
With a glory in His bosom that transfigures you and me;
As He died to make men holy, let us live to make men free,
While God is marching on.

He is coming like the glory of the morning on the wave;
He is wisdom to the mighty, He is honor to the brave;
So the world shall be His footstool, and the soul of wrong
His slave.
Our God is marching on.

Glory! Glory, Hallelujah!
Glory! Glory, Hallelujah!
Glory! Glory, Hallelujah!
Our God is marching on.

America—My Country, 'Tis of Thee

Words: Samuel L. Smith
Music: *Thesaurus Musicus*

My country 'tis of thee,
Sweet land of liberty,
Of thee I sing:
Land where my fathers died,
Land of the pilgrims' pride,
From every mountainside
Let freedom ring!

My native country thee,
Land of the noble free,
Thy name I love:
I love thy rocks and rills,
Thy woods and templed hills;
My heart with rapture thrills,
Like thee above.

Let music swell the breeze,
And ring from all the trees,
Sweet freedom's song;
Let mortal tongues awake;
Let all that breathe partake;
Let rocks their silence break,
The sound prolong.

Our fathers' God, to Thee,
Author of liberty,
To Thee we sing;
Long may our land be bright
With freedom's holy light;
Protect us by Thy might;
Great God, our King!

"We hold these truths to be self evident. That all men are created equal, that they are endowed by their Creator with certain unalienable rights, that among these are life, liberty, and the pursuit of happiness."

The Star-Spangled Banner

Words: Francis Scott Key
Music: *John Stafford Smith*

Oh! say, can you see,
by the dawn's early light,
What so proudly we hailed
at the twilight's last gleaming?
Whose broad stripes and bright
stars, through the perilous flight,
O'er the ramparts we watched
were so gallantly streaming?
And the rockets red glare,
the bombs bursting in air
Gave proof through the night
that our flag was still there.
Oh! say, does that star-
spangled banner yet wave
O'er the land of the free
and the home of the brave?

On the shore, dimly seen
through the mist of the deep,
Where the foe's haughty host
in dread silence reposes,
What is that which the breeze,
o'er the towering steep,
As it fitfully blows, half
conceals, half discloses?
Now it catches the gleam
of the morning's first beam,
In full glory reflected,
now shines on the stream.
'Tis the star-spangled banner.
Oh! long may it wave
O'er the land of the free
and the home of the brave!

And where is that band
who so vauntingly swore
That the havoc of war and the
battle's confusion
A home and a country should
leave us no more?
Their blood has washed out
their foul footstep's pollution.
No refuge could save the
hireling and slave
From the terror of flight or the
gloom of the grave,
And the star-spangled banner
in triumph doth wave
O'er the land of the free
and the home of the brave.

Oh! thus be it ever
when freemen shall stand
Between their loved home and
the war's desolation,
Blest with vict'ry and peace,
may the Heav'n-rescued land
Praise the Pow'r that hath
made and preserved us a
nation.
Then conquer we must, when
our cause it is just, And this
be our motto - "**God is our
trust.**"
And the star-spangled banner
in triumph shall wave
O'er the land of the free
and the home of the brave.

America the Beautiful

Words: Katharine Lee Bates
Music: Samuel A. Ward

O beautiful for spacious skies,
For amber waves of grain,
For purple mountain majesties
Above the fruited plain!
America! America! *God shed His grace on thee,*
And crown thy good with brotherhood
From sea to shining sea.

O beautiful for pilgrim feet,
Whose stern impassioned stress,
A thoroughfare for freedom beat
Across the wilderness!
America! America! *God mend thine every flaw,*
Confirm thy soul in self control,
They liberty in law.

O beautiful for heroes proved
In liberating strife,
Who more than self their country loved,
And mercy more than life!
America! America! *May God thy gold refine,*
Till all success be nobleness,
And every gain divine.

O beautiful for patriot dream
That sees, beyond the years,
Thine alabaster cities gleam,
Undimmed by human tears!
America! America! *God shed His grace on thee,*
And crown thy good with brotherhood
From sea to shining sea.

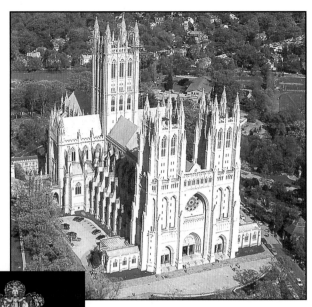

Washington National Cathedral

"A great church for national purpose . . . equally open to all." Begun in 1907, the building was finished in 1990. Funerals and memorial services for many national heros have been held there.

Chapels within the cathedral have provided parish homes for Polish, Russo-Carpathian, Syrian, and Serbian Orthodox churches. Martin Luther King, Jr., preached his last Sunday sermon from the cathedral's pulpit. Washington National Cathedral may well be the last great Gothic building to be attempted anywhere in the world.

Children are the living messages
we send to a time we will not see.

THE PRESENT

"People have forgotten God."

—Solzhenitsyn

"I don't like these cold, precise, perfect people who, in order not to speak wrong, never speak at all, in order not to do wrong, never do anything."
—Rev. Henry Ward Beecher

Since the birth of the Constitution, the *First Amendment* has been misunderstood and misquoted. Ask the average person on the street what it states and the vast majority will reply it says something about a "wall of separation between church and state."

Of course, that is not what it says at all. Jefferson's innocent, passing phrase has become, in the minds of perhaps most Americans, a substitute for the *First Amendment*, which spells out the role of religion in a Democratic Republic.

The *First Amendment* limits what Congress may do. It was written so that people would have full protection of their rights to free and unrestricted worship. But we have seen in our day a 180-degree turn from what the *First Amendment* says. Liberals and secular humanists proclaim that somehow the *First Amendment's* purpose is to protect the government from the influence *of* religion![1]

"If my people, who are called by my name will humble themselves and pray and seek my face and turn from their wicked ways, then will I hear from heaven and will forgive their sin and will heal their land."

—2 Chronicles 7:14

"When the foundations are being destroyed, what can the righteous do?"

—Psalm 11:3

The current interpretations of the *First Amendment* are not the product of constitutional intent, but of a bewildering array of Supreme Court decisions with a tendency to secularize the public life of the nation and to work a restrained but taxing persecution on Christians and other people of faith who want to integrate their faith with their public life.

The American religious consensus has been eroded. The Supreme Court left "under God" in the *Pledge of Allegiance* in 1963. Justice William Brennan wrote it could be kept in the pledge only because the words "no longer have a religious purpose or meaning" but merely recognizes "the historical fact that our nation was believed to have been founded under God."[2]

Since 1940, the Supreme Court has prohibited schools from composing a prayer to recite before class[3] and stripped the Ten Commandments from the classroom bulletin board.[4]

Liberal Revisionism Verses Historical Fact

"If men and nations would but live by the precepts of the ancient prophets and the teachings of the Sermon on the Mount, problems which now seem so difficult would soon disappear . . . Oh, for an Isaiah or a St. Paul to reawaken a sick world to its moral responsibilities."
—President Harry S. Truman, 1946

For two hundred years, America functioned, grew, and prospered under the tacit agreement that America was a religious country, without demanding allegiance to a specific church. Congress opened with a prayer and the Ten Commandments were posted on courtroom and schoolroom walls. God was always invoked in presidential speeches and community events. The assumption was that all Americans were "one nation under God." Religion in general had a respective place in our nation's affairs and Christianity, in particular, was a positive undercurrent.[5]

But today, we hear over and over again that Christianity must be kept out of public policy and this was the original intent of our ancestors. In 1996, the American Jewish Committee stated:

"The religious right may be convincing people that this country was founded on religious principles, and that the founders intended to create a Christian nation, since the religious rictus keep saying that. We must continue to publicize our view of American history and make it relevant to people today."[6]

If two neighbors quarrel as to whether Mt. Rainier or Mt. Fuji is higher, it is easy to determine, since they can consult an atlas to ascertain which is correct. If one American feels that Van Gogh is a superior painter to Rembrandt, there may never be an agreement. In fact, there is no correct answer to the debate.

As Americans, we can never resolve whether Christianity, Judaism or any other religion is the true expression of God's will. Religion is an area where we must each respect the other's right to believe differently than ourselves.

Problems of the relationship between church and state bedevil this generation. Communicating about the matters that touch the inner most fabric of belief, religious or irreligious, and the depth of church-state relationships in this nation requires communication among all of us. We must talk *with* one another, not at one another. We need more dialogue and less diatribe.

Justice Black's opinion for the U.S. Supreme Court in *Everson*[7] and *McCollum*[8] speaks resolutely of a "wall between church and state which must be kept high and impregnable."[9]

The wall metaphor was also used by Martin Luther when he accused "Romanists" of having drawn "three walls 'round themselves, with which they have hitherto protected themselves, so that no one could reform them."[10]

But the wall is not an accurate means of describing the relationship between church and state.[11]

Only the most narrow separationists would contend that religion, which played such a major role in the establishment of this country and which occupies such an important place in the actions and thinking of so many of its citizens, should not have an honorable place in our public life.[12]

The dangers of the subject of religion in our school curriculum has been so great that irreligious people would abolish all mention of God and religion in the public schools. The complete elimination of religion from the curriculum of a school that is seeking to teach moral values amounts to an establishment of secular humanism.

Irreligion demands the protection of the Free Exercise Clause, but the irreligious must be equally willing to accept the prescriptions of non-establishment.[13]

When we debate whether or not this country was founded on religious principles, there is a tremendous volume of material from which to draw. **Secular liberal groups are attempting to rewrite American history and in many cases, have begun to succeed. It is a clever strategy.**

Historical Logic

"America was born a Christian nation. America was born to exemplify that devotion to the elements of righteousness which are derived from the revelations of the holy scriptures."
—**Woodrow Wilson, May 7, 1911**

"It cannot be emphasized too strongly or too often that this great nation was founded, not by religionists but by Christians; not on religions, but on the Gospel of Jesus Christ. For this very reason, people of other faiths have been afforded asylum, prosperity, and freedom of worship here."
—**Patrick Henry (1736–1799)**

"A page of history is worth a volume of logic."
—**Justice Oliver Wendell Holmes (1841–1932)**

Whether the *First Amendment* is read as supporting a strict separationist or accommodationist position, it is clear that history cannot be disregarded.

U.S. Supreme Court Justice William Brennan appealed to history to support his interpretation of the *Bill of Rights*, that the line to be drawn between permissible and impermissible involvements of religion and public life is "one which accords with history and faithfully reflects the understanding of the Founding Fathers."

Pledge of Allegiance

Contrary to the ACLU, Freedom From Religion, Inc., and Americans United for Separation of Church and State, which argue for a strict separationist view, the *First Amendment* was intended to maintain a proper relationship between government and religion. There is no high or impregnable wall of separation between church and state. There never has been! The state must affirmatively accommodate and even "aid" religion in certain circumstances.

History proves the revolutionary and founding periods of American history favored governmental accommodation of religious practice. Both Jefferson and Madison, often cited for their disestablishmentarianism, in fact, approved numerous religious practices in public life. Indeed, they participated in legislative activities on behalf of religion that would disturb the very strict separationists who cite Jefferson and Madison in support of strict separationism.

In 1785, Madison introduced in the Virginia House of Delegates five bills touching upon religion which Jefferson had assumed the responsibility for drafting.

The unfortunate consequence of some of the *First Amendment* cases is that "the Court has widened the gap between current social reality and current constitutional law."

"An examination of the early activities of the Federal Government indicates that the people approved and welcomed its aid to church-related activities . . . there was undoubtedly the faith that subsequent generations of Americans would be able to utilize the power of the federal government to promote the concurrent interests of government and religion under First Amendment norms that were reasonable, pragmatic, and just."[14]

Jefferson expressed his views on church and state more clearly a few years after his famous letter in his Second Inaugural Address in 1805:

"In matters of religion I have considered that its free exercise is placed by the Constitution independent of the powers of the general [federal] government. I have, therefore, undertaken on no occasion to prescribe the religious exercises suited to it, but have left them, as the Constitution found them, under the direction and discipline of the state or church authorities acknowledged by the several religious societies."

He and other framers mistrusted the federal government and feared any attempt it might make to establish a national church. Religion was to be a state concern, not a federal one.

The term *establishment of religion* was to prevent a national church.

"It was never intended by the Constitution that the government should be prohibited from recognizing religion, or that religious worship should never be provided for in cases where a proper recognition of divine providence in the working of the government might seem to require it, and where it might be done without drawing any invidious distinctions between differing religious beliefs, organizations, or sects. The Christian religion was always recognized in the administration of the common law, and so far that the law continues to be the law of the land, the fundamental principles of that religion must continue to be recognized in the same cases and to the same extent as formerly."[15]

One historian noted:

"To Jefferson, the wall of separation did not mean the complete and absolute separation of church and state such that no religion or religious influence was to be permitted in state-sponsored activities and laws. His chief aim was not the erection of an impenetrable wall of separation. Rather, it was the protection of free expression of one's religious beliefs and opinions. And if that goal was best achieved through statutory cooperation between church and state, Jefferson appeared willing to endorse it."

Supreme Court

In public schools, and society at large, the Supreme Court has omitted from its version of history Thomas Jefferson's many actions that contradict his strict separationist reputation focusing on the image of a "high and impregnable wall" between separation of church and state.

Religious Expression in Public Schools

"The only foundation for useful education in a republic is to be laid in Religion. Without this there can never be virtue, and without virtue, there can never be liberty, and liberty is the object and life of all the republican governments."
—**Benjamin Rush, (1745–1813)**

The *Northwest Ordinance* of 1787, which set aside federal property for schools states:

"Religion, morality, and knowledge being necessary to good government and the happiness of mankind, schools and the meaning of learning shall forever be encouraged."

Textbooks referred to God without embarrassment, and public schools considered their major task to be the development of character through the teaching of religion. The *New England Primer* opened with certain religious admonitions followed by the Lord's Prayer, the Apostles' Creed, the Ten Commandments, and the names of the Books of the Bible.

The "Free Exercise" of Religion Clause

Recent attempts to limit public religious expression have also occurred. There are groups and individuals whose goal of a secular society is clearly threatened by the mention of God or Jesus Christ. They do what they can to diminish the improving public climate towards religion. They do what they have always done: misportray, distort, and/or ignore the truth. Those who have become particularly skillful at this are termed "historical revisionists," causing courts to micromanage religious expressions.[16]

The ultimate goal of these organizations is to drive churches further out of public view. Eventually, the mere view (from a public street) of a cross upon a church steeple may be claimed to cause "emotional distress" and thus constitute "injury."

The Supreme Court has changed its interpretation with regards to the application of the Free Exercise Clause.

Prior to 1990, the applicable test was:

1. There must be a sincerely held religious belief negatively impacted or burdened by some government role regulation.
2. The government must have a compelling governmental interest for the restriction.
3. The government must achieve its interest in the least restrictive means available.[17]

After 1990, the Supreme Court weakened the test:

1. Any law that is generally applicable, and
2. Neutral in application.[18]

The stricter standard that applied prior to 1990 will be used only if the law is found to specifically target religion,[19] or if the *First Amendment* Free Exercise Clause can be combined with some other constitutional violation.

God has blessed America. Over the past 200 years, under His guidance, America has risen to levels and achievements attained by few other nations in the history of the world. Yet notice how we have responded to Him in recent years. **In a nation once distinguished for its faith and made great by its people of faith, public expressions of that traditional faith are now viewed as a threat to government.**

The "Establishment" Clause

The strict purpose of the Establishment Clause was never to require a "strict neutrality between religion and non-religion." It was designed to prohibit Congress from establishing a national church or designating a particular faith or sect above the rest.

The word *religion*, in the Founder's *First Amendment* discussions, was used to mean a single Christian denomination. That is a fact made evident by the dozen or so different iterations of the *First Amendment*, which they, themselves, proposed. The original version, proposed in the Senate on September 3, 1789, stated, "Congress will not make any law establishing any religious denomination." The second version stated, "Congress shall make no law establishing any particular denomination." The third version is very similar; it said, "Congress shall make no law establishing any particular denomination in preference to others." The word religion was interchangeable with the word *denomination*.

According to the Congressional records, on September 20th, 1789, Fisher Aimes was the Founding Father who offered the final wording for the *First Amendment*. Aimes expressed concern that as more textbooks were being introduced in the school classrooms, the Bible might drift to the back of the classroom. He warned this could never be allowed in America and that the Bible must always remain the number one textbook in our schools. Aimes concluded by stressing the Bible is the source of sound morality and behavior in America.

The debate over the "jurisprudence of original intention" causes law schools, think tanks, judicial conferences, and political gatherings to debate the *First Amendment*.[20]

The Establishment Clause has two basic interpretations as to what our framers intended it to mean: (1) the broad interpretation and (2) the narrow interpretation.[19]

The *narrow* view prohibits a national church, or passing a law to prefer one faith over another. It was extended no further than a prohibition against the government's recognition of an official church or the favoring of one religion over another.

The first Congress, many of whom being members of the Philadelphia convention and various state ratifying conventions, were well aware what the clause was intended to mean and never thought the wall of separation between church and state was to be a severe or complete wall. The application of the *Bill of Rights* to the states in this regard has done "much to alter the moral tone of communities across the country."[21]

The *broad approach* in a strict separation is that no church or religious group should ever receive any governmental aid.

In light of the dizzy state of Supreme Court cases, it is fair to ask, "Where are we headed?" Officially, the Supreme Court yardstick for testing the absence of an Establishment Clause violation is the Lemon[22] three-part test, that is, the legislation in question is not deemed an establishment of religion if it: (1) has a secular purpose, (2) neither advances nor inhibits religion, (3) and does not cause an excessive entanglement between religion and government.

The Parties. There must be a governmental party and a private party. The *First Amendment* restrains government on the one hand and protects the private liberty of the individual on the other hand.

There is no *First Amendment* application if the adversarial parties are merely private. One must be a governmental actor and one must be a private actor.

The Forum. The three forums include the traditional public forum, a limited or designated public forum, and a non-public forum.[23]

A traditional public forum includes a street, sidewalk, or park. A limited, or designated, public forum is one in which any public facility is intentionally opened to the public by the government for expressive activity. An example of such a forum which is used by private groups is a public school that is used by private groups during non-school hours. A non-public forum is public property which the government has not intentionally opened for expressive activity. An example is a utility pole or a public airport.

The Restrictions. The third step is to identify the type of restraint. The various kinds of restraint include: a content-neutral restraint, a content-based restraint, a viewpoint restraint, and a prior restraint.

A *content-neutral restraint* is a governmental restriction on speech that does not attempt to restrict the content of the message. An example is a parade permit, which permits all applicants to specify the designated time and route of the parade. Such a requirement is applicable to all speech regardless of the content.

A *content-based restraint* is a restriction on a specific category of speech such as where the government permits political speech but attempts to restrict religious speech.

A *viewpoint restraint* is one where the government allows political speech but only from the Democratic rather than the Republican viewpoint.

Prior restraint is a restriction on speech before it occurs. One example is where the government requires the speaker to obtain prior permission to speak.

The Test. Once the actors, the forum, and the restriction are identified, the applicable test can also be identified and then applied.

The Establishment Clause test has gone through several variations. Many members of the Supreme Court in the past years have criticized the widely-used three-part *Lemon* Test and the Court does not always use it.[24]

The key is to have some secular purpose along with the religious purpose.

Once during a graduation prayer case, the Court used a *coercion test*,[25] and once, when considering legislative prayers, the court used no test at all but instead looked to the *original intent* and the history surrounding the *First Amendment*.[26]

The *Lemon* Test has three parts:
1. There must be a secular purpose;
2. The government action must not primarily promote, endorse, or inhibit religion;
3. The government action must not foster excessive governmental entanglement with religion.

If the government fails any one of the three prongs of the test, then the governmental action will be considered unconstitutional.

Under the first prong, there need only be a secular purpose, although there may also be a religious purpose. The key is to have some secular purpose along with the religious purpose.

Under the second prong, the government may not primarily endorse, promote, or inhibit religion.

Under the third prong, the government may not become excessively entangled with religion. If a Christmas nativity scene sponsored by the government on public property displays Baby Jesus, then it is unconstitutional. This is so because it only has a religious purpose and not a secular one. *However*, if within the same context of a religious nativity scene the government also displays a secular symbol of the holiday such as Santa Claus, reindeer, or a Christmas tree, then the Supreme Court will consider the display to have a secular purpose. The entire context of the display does not have the primary purpose of endorsing or promoting religion. Although religion is evident, it is not the primary purpose of the display and there is no excessive governmental entanglement because the administration or maintenance of the display requires very little government involvement.

The same is true for religious Christmas carols in the public school. If students sing only Christian Christmas carols during a Christmas pageant, then the pageant is a violation of the Establishment Clause. However, if secular songs such *Rudolph, the Red-Nosed Reindeer* are also sung alongside *Silent Night, Holy Night*, then the presentation is constitutional. This is because the secular songs create a secular purpose. While some songs endorse and promote religion, the entire pageant does not primarily endorse or promote religion because of the secular songs. Finally, there is very little government entanglement since the government is actually neutral by celebrating both the secular and sacred aspects of the holiday.[27]

Judicial scholars agree that there are "no clear guidelines as to how the Clause should be interpreted." Should there be a hardline separationist "no aid" approach such as *Everson*,[28] *McCollum*,[29] and *Engel*,[30] or a more flexible, accommodationist "no preference" approach as under *Zorach v Clausen*,[29] used more out of convenience than commitment, and provide "no more than a helpful signpost" in dealing with Establishment Clause challenges.[31]

There is some suggestion that the prohibitions in the federal *Bill of Rights* might be applied to the states. In 1810, Chief Justice John Marshall suggested:

> "The Constitution of the United States contains what may be deemed a Bill of Rights for the people of each state."[32]

But in 1833, the great Chief Justice removed any question as to the applicability of the *Bill of Rights* when he wrote:

> "These amendments contain no expression indicating an intention to apply them to the State Governments. This Court cannot so apply them."[33]

The adoption of the *Fourteenth Amendment* (1868) forbids states to "make or enforce any law which shall abridge the privileges or immunities of citizens of the United States," or to "deprive any person of life, liberty, or property without due process of law."

No "in toto incorporation" was adopted until 1940 during one of the leading Jehovah's Witnesses cases, *Cantwell v Connecticut.*[34]

The Justices of the Supreme Court have, on occasion, appealed to the intention of the authors of the *Constitution* in arriving at their decision, but there is no unanimity about what the authors had in mind when they composed the clause.

> "Historical data can throw some light on the purposes behind such language, but all too often intention of the framers has been a rhetorical device employed by partisans to read their own policy preferences into the Constitution."[35]

All was quiet along the wall until *Everson v Board of Education,*[35] which has since assumed massive proportions and has been growing ever since. Its growth has been largely literary and ornamental.[36]

> "The wall has no future. What has a future is the rational, non-metaphorical discussion in the light of all the provisions of the First Amendment, of the methods by which we may guarantee and promote religious freedom, and the methods by which we may obtain an educational system worthy of the potentialities and responsibilities of our people . . . the First Amendment is not intended as a fence, or wall, around a vacant lot. Something is supposed to be going on inside. What is supposed to be going on is learning. A political community is an education life in process. The wall has no future because it cannot help us learn."[37]

In *Everson,* a strict separationist position on church-state matters was taken. By 1963, the court characterized its view of the Establishment Clause as "long established." The wall of separation metaphor was written years later after the *Constitution* became the touchstone for interpreting the Establishment Clause.

By 1985, the court was no longer relying on the intent of the framers when it struck down an Alabama law providing a moment of silence for meditation or prayer.[38] Justice Stevens acknowledged that the Establishment Clause had a different meaning "at one time."

Justice William H. Rehnquist has provided us complete review of a historical record as to the intent of the framers of the *First Amendment.* In words similar to those of Judge Hand, Rehnquist challenged the court's history as "totally incorrect":

> ". . . that the Establishment Clause of the First Amendment had acquired a well-accepted meaning: it forbade establishment of a national religion, and forbade preference among religious sects or denominations . . . the Establishment Clause did not require government neutrality between religion and irreligion, nor did it prohibit the federal government from providing non-discriminatory aid to religion. There is simply no historical foundation for the position that the Framers intended to build the 'wall of separation' that was constitutionalized in *Everson.*"

The language of the *First Amendment* never created a wall of separation between church and state.[39]

Chief Justice Rehnquist declared:

> "The well-accepted meaning of the Establishment Clause is that it merely prohibited the establishment of a national church. It created no wall of separation between church and state. It did not require government neutrality between religion and irreligion . . ."

Lynch v Donnelly (1984)[40]

In a landmark U.S. Supreme Court decision, the City of Pawtucket, Rhode Island, was allowed to erect a nativity scene. A creche was displayed in a park owned by a non-profit organization in the heart of a shopping district. The traditional figures of the infant Jesus, Mary and Joseph, angels, shepherds, kings and animals were all *maintained by the city*. The American Civil Liberties Union challenged the city's inclusion of the creche in the annual display.

The Court admitted that the real and substantial effect of affiliating the city with the Christian beliefs that the creche represents, gives the appearance of official sponsorship and confirms more than a remote and incidental benefit on Christianity.

But more importantly, the Court, once and for all, put aside the notion of a strict separation of church and state. The Court held the *Constitution does not require complete separation of church and state, but affirmatively mandates accommodation, not merely tolerance, of all religions, and forbids hostility towards any.* **Anything less than accommodation of all religions would require *"callous indifference"* which was never intended by the Establishment Clause of the *First Amendment*.**

To forbid the use of a nativity scene as part of the city's annual Christmas display at the time people were taking note of the season with Christmas hymns and carols in public schools and other public places, and while Congress and legislatures open sessions with prayers by paid chaplains, would be "stilted overreaction." It would be ironic if the inclusion of the symbol of a particular historic religious event, as part of a celebration acknowledged in the Western World for twenty centuries, and in this country by the people, the Executive Branch, Congress, and the courts for two centuries, would so "taint" the city's exhibit as to render it violative of the Establishment Clause.

The Court acknowledged "fears and political problems" that gave rise to the Religion Clause of the *First Amendment* are of far less concern today. Any notion that a creche would pose a real danger of establishment of a state church is far-fetched, indeed. It is far too late in the day to *"impose a crabbed reading of the Clause on the country."*

If there are any remaining believers in a *strict* separation of church and state, it is only because they refuse to read and understand American law.

While America Played

"The frustrating thing is that those who are attacking religion claim they are doing it in the name of tolerance, freedom, and open-mindedness. Question: Isn't the real truth that they are intolerant of religion? They refuse to tolerate its importance in their lives."

—President Ronald Reagan[41]
(1911–   )

"The safest road to Hell is the gradual one—the gentle slope, soft under foot, without sudden turnings, without milestones, without signposts."

—C. S. Lewis (1898–1963)
The Screwtape Letters

In 1925, the teaching of Bible creation was taken from our public schools and replaced with the teaching of evolution.

In 1948, religious instruction was stopped in most public schools.

In 1962, prayer and Bible reading were taken from school children.

In 1973, babies were killed before they were born.

In 1978, the singing of Christmas carols was stopped in many schools.

In 1980, the Ten Commandments were stripped from the walls of school classrooms.

In 1981, crosses were removed from city parks.

In 1982, a house of worship was padlocked in Louisville, Nebraska, and the pastor jailed.

In 1983, many school children were stopped from carrying their own Bibles to school and were forbidden to say "grace" before their meals.

In 1984, public school teachers started dropping the words "under God" from the Pledge of Allegiance, and in other schools the American flag was removed from the classroom.

What has America come to? Where have our freedoms gone? And who is to blame? More importantly, how can we get them back?

When the *Constitution* was written and tempers exploded as delegates were ready to go back to their respective colonies after an unsuccessful attempt to write the *Constitution, Benjamin Franklin* called that First Continental Congress together and *asked men to get down on their knees on the floor of Constitutional Hall and ask for God's guidance and God's help in the writing of the Constitution.* When they came up off their knees, they wrote one of the greatest documents of all time in America. It was written after a prayer meeting.

Historian Roger Babson said many years ago:

"People went to South America in search of gold, but they came to North America in search of God."

As our spiritual leadership and foundations are weakened in America, so is America itself weakened. Two hundred years ago Edmund Burke (1729–1797) said:

"The only thing necessary for evil to triumph is for good men to do nothing."

Many teachers in our colleges and universities do not believe the Bible anymore. They mock the Word of God. It is called a book of folklore, legend, and stories handed down across the years. Many teachers sneeringly tell their students they are atheists. They use profane language and sometimes set bad examples before the students.

There is a God to cuss by, but no God to pray to! Our responsibility begins with our youth:

"Train up a child in the way he should go, and when he is old he will not depart from it."
—Proverbs 22:6

If we make a mockery of God or of the faith of our Founding Fathers, then we deny ourselves the legacy we enjoy as Americans.

Founding Fathers

Our interpretations of history are based on our own "world view" which is our way of viewing or interpreting all of reality. We are witnessing a great struggle today for the heart and soul of our nation, a battle between two competing world views.[42]

Our founding fathers believed in the *Biblical world view*. They believed in the inherently evil nature of man and in absolute truth. It was a tradition to read the *Declaration of Independence* every July 4th to remind people of the cost of freedom.

The opposite *post-modern world view* now dominates our culture. This view believes there is no absolute truth and man is inherently good. The presence of evil in the world is due to a problem in man's environment. If the environment is fixed, then evil will disappear. All truth is relative and open to change.

- **John Quincy Adams** spoke on the steps of the Capital explaining that revolutionary America was able to throw off external constraints of the British government because the citizens were bound by the *laws of God*.
- **Benjamin Franklin** noticed that children don't have to be taught how to misbehave since it comes naturally. He said, "Only a virtuous people are capable of freedom. As nations become corrupt and vicious, they have more need of masters."
- **James Madison** in *Federalist Paper 51* said, "If men were angels, no government would be necessary."
- **Noah Webster** said: "In selecting men for office, look to his character. If citizens neglect their duty and place unprincipled men in office, the government will soon be corrupted. When the citizen gives his vote to a man of known immorality, he betrays the interest of his country."

- The 1787 *Northwest Ordinance* established a government for the territory that eventually became the states of Ohio, Indiana, Illinois, Michigan and Wisconsin. *Dealing With Education*, Article III states: "Religion, morality and knowledge being necessary to good government and the happiness of mankind, schools and a means of education shall forever be encouraged."

- According to the *Science of Government Textbook* (1841), religion was the foundation of law and justice. As a created being, man is subject to the laws of his Creator.

- In the *New England Primer* (1790), all teachers are directed to: "Train up a child in the way he will go, and when he is grown, he will not depart from it."

- **Alexis de Tocqueville** stated: "The Americans combined the notion of Christianity and liberty so eminently in their minds that it is impossible to make them conceive the one without the other. When these men attack religious opinions, they obey the dictates of their passions but not of their interests. . . . Despotism may govern without faith, but liberty cannot."

Today's Textbooks

Today's textbooks filter much of American history through the lens of a post-modern world view.

A current popular eighth grade textbook, *A More Perfect Union*, in a section titled "Change Without Amendment," students are taught the Supreme Court can change the *Constitution* without following the amendment procedure. This is called the "unofficial method." The *Constitution* may thus be re-interpreted depending upon the views of the new Justices. Therefore, judicial activism is inevitable and our law is no longer grounded in original intent.

In *America Will Be*, a fifth grade social studies book, the teacher is told to: "Explain how the tension created by dissenters may have led to the Salem persecution of women accused of witchcraft."

The persecution of women was the purpose behind the witchhunts instead of the fear of witchcraft. Ministers may have especially wanted to keep in line any outspoken women who challenged male authority.

"Ask students to think of a law they would like to see passed. Suggest environment, endangered species, and education . . . have students produce a bill of rights for animals. Tell them to begin by discussing the ways in which they feel animals have been treated unfairly."

Is this not clear evidence of social engineering?

In *A More Perfect Union*, the only mention of John Quincy Adams is that: "Adams stood for the old Republican values. He represented the ruling elite, the wealthy, and the well educated. He was known as a harsh, stubborn person. He was not a strong leader because he received no popular support from the people."

Censored out of the textbook was the fact that at the age of 14 he received a Congressional appointment as Secretary to the Ambassador to the Court of Catherine the Great in Russia. He was U.S. Minister to France. As U.S. Minister to Britain he negotiated the Treaty of Ghent ending the War of 1812. He was Secretary of State under President Monroe and re-elected to the legislature for 18 consecutive years after his term as our sixth President. Was this a President that "received no popular support from the people?"

Adams led the fight to lift the gag rule which prohibited discussion of slavery earning him the nickname of the "hell hound of slavery." When asked why he continued to fight such an unpopular fight, he said, "Duty is ours, results belong to God." But, of course, as a dedicated Christian he was harsh and stubborn.

Sam Adams was a patriot, member of the Continental Congress, and a signer of the *Declaration of Independence*. He is given little mention in today's textbooks. A textbook states that he "whipped up crowds of protest and wrote inflammatory newspaper articles," but it has omitted that he wrote regarding the rights of Colonists such things as: "The right to freedom being the gift of the Almighty, the rights of the Colonists as Christians may be best understood by reading and carefully studying the institution of the Great Law Giver and Head of the Christian Church which are to be found clearly written and promulgated in the New Testament."

A More Perfect Union describes the Revolution as a "destructive civil war" in which patriots jeered their loyalists neighbors and vandalized and burned their houses. They took the law into their own hands to find and harass loyalists, burned settlements and crops, and committed "brutal acts against civilians, driving many settlers from their homes."

In *The World Past and Present*, by MacMillan, Lenin and Communist parties merely want ". . . the nation to be wealthy enough to satisfy all people without coercion." The book idealizes Mao Tse-Tung as being a leader who "recognized the needs of the poor."

It has been said that Fidel Castro has made "life better under Castro's Communist dictatorship, and there is less poverty since Castro gained control."

There are repeated attacks on historical truths. Contemporary textbooks distort historical facts replacing them with carefully worded ideas that greatly change the nature of history and that of the world. All references to Judeo-Christian foundations of our country are censored. The post-modernist uses their version of historical events to bring about significant change in the attitudes and beliefs of today's students.

Tolerance in Government

In today's era dominated by the new tolerance, Christians must keep in mind facts about the Founder of our faith:

1. From the moment of His birth, He was considered a political threat. (Matt. 2:16–18).

2. He and His earliest followers were members of an oft-oppressed people ruled by a colonial power;

3. He was executed by the state (Matt. 27:27–31).

For centuries, Christians around the world have followed in the steps of Jesus and have been imprisoned, martyred, and faced persecution and discrimination.

Christians in America, however, have enjoyed a general freedom from such conditions, but the consensus that once governed the public and private life in our nation has crumbled to the point where we now live in a post-Christian society. We now live in a society where the Christian faith is often dismissed or ridiculed—Christians are considered suspect and their motives berated.[43]

We are "in the world" but not "of the world." Christians have answered this question in various ways with varying success:

- Strict separationists—A complete non-religious state with the separation of religion from all civil matters.
- Pluralistic separationists—A neutral state, but will still use religious values to influence government.
- Institutional separationists—Benevolent neutrality toward Judeo-Christian religious values.
- Non-preferentialists—The government maintains a strong interest in preserving and fostering faith in the best interests of the public as a basis for morality.
- Restorationists—Actively working to restore Christianity to the status they believe it held in early America, and want to see the country become a Christian nation again.[44]

As Christians, we have a dual citizenship. Our greatest and most lasting victory will not be achieved in Washington or any of our state capitols, but in the Cross of Calvary.

It was perfectly evident to all, including early Jewish-Americans, that there was no threat in our nation's Christian orientation. Christmas was to be a national holiday. No one argued that the

Post Office or other government offices should be open on Christmas for fear of non-Christians.

Let's be honest—most of us would rather have a next-door neighbor whose practical, day-to-day values correspond to our own—even if his theology and faith are different. Worship as you will, as long as your behavior and values reflect the basic ethic of the Judeo-Christian tradition; then we are well off.

We are fortunate to live in a society whose government is not committed to any particular theology, but which is committed to a broad Judeo-Christian understanding of good and evil in human behavior.

More homes per capita in America possess a Bible than in any other country in the world. More Americans attend regular worship services than in any other industrialized nation. More Americans say a prayer before meals than in any other western country.[45]

"That Book, Sir, is the rock on which our republic rests."

—**Andrew Jackson, June 8, 1845**
(1767–1845)

Today many high school and college students could easily be led to believe that our founding fathers were more concerned with freedom *from* religion rather than religious freedom. Without a doubt, this nation was founded by Christians and was meant to be based on broad Christian principles. Religion was the bedrock upon which our nation stood and without it, these amazing men and women saw no future for the country they had established.

There was an unprecedented respect for tolerance of Judaism. Historical records clearly show there were Jews, some of them prominent, in the American colonies. They participated in the Revolutionary War and were certainly known to the Founding Fathers.

Revisionist History

"I believe the next half-century will determine if we will advance the cause of Christian civilization or revert to the horrors of brutal paganism."
—President Theodore Roosevelt (1912)

During the past 25 years, early American history has been rewritten. This generation of public school students can go through 12 years of elementary and high school and another four years of college without one lesson featuring the central role of America's Judeo-Christian heritage in the founding of the nation.

In 1986, a study of the public school textbooks in America found religion in our history to be "largely excised." Former Secretary of Education, William J. Bennett, denounced this as an "assault of secularism on religion." The study illustrates how there is a liberal bias of the courts to "skirt controversy." There is not any "serious positive treatment to conservative views," since school textbooks fail to mention God. The religious faith and biblical heritage of our forefathers have been eliminated from the record almost all together.

It's mind-boggling. An overwhelming majority of elementary and high school textbooks go to extraordinary lengths to avoid *any* references to religion. Some American history books define Pilgrims as "people who take long trips" or define fundamentalists as "rural people who followed the values and traditions of an earlier period . . ."

Many textbooks study the Pilgrim's first Thanksgiving Day without any reference to their thanking God for their survival in the new land.

The central role of Christian faith in shaping the charters of our original colonies has been censored from this historical record.

We should not forget the heroic contributions to the exploration and settling of the New World by Christian missionaries, ministers, priests, and laity over the past 2,500 years. The courage and self-sacrificing efforts of those early missionaries to plant churches, schools, hospitals, orphanages, clinics, and every kind of spiritual and social service throughout the world is crucial. Understanding the facts of our history is the only way we can wisely chart the nation's future.

Has the very mention of God's name in public become an offense? Have we come to the point where it is now considered wrong to acknowledge the name of God at all?

Even Norman Lear's liberal People for the American Way said "with only rare exceptions," American history textbooks for junior high school students "treat religion by exclusion or by brief and simplistic reference."

From Sam Adams to Patrick Henry, to Benjamin Franklin to

The First Thanksgiving

Alexander Hamilton, all the Founders intended religion to provide a moral anchor for our liberty in democracy. All would be puzzled were they to return to modern America today and find among certain elite circles in the academy and the media, a scorn for public expression of religious values that clashes directly with the Founders' vision of religion as a friend of civic life.

It is ironic that anyone who appeals to religious values today runs the risk of being called "divisive" or attacked as an enemy of pluralism, tolerance, diversity, or multi-culturalism. American culture and American greatness draws strength and direction from the Judeo-Christian tradition. The religion of our people is not a risk to America.

Distinguished constitutional historian Edward S. Corwin stated:

". . . the historical record shows beyond pre-adventure that the core of an establishment of religion comprises the idea of preference; and that any act of public authority favorable to religion in general cannot, without manifest falsification of history, be brought under the ban of that phrase."

First Baptist Meeting House

"Our democracy is intertwined (entangled) with the vitality of the Judeo-Christian tradition. This tradition is not a source of fear in the world; it is a ground of hope. No one demands adherence to any particular religious belief as a condition of citizenship or as a proof of good citizenship but still, we should not deny what is true, that from the Judeo-Christian tradition come our values, our principles, and the spirit of our institutions. That tradition is entangled and wed together.

If we have disdain for our religious tradition, we have disdain for ourselves."

Proof That Separation of Church/State Is a Lie

"Man, considered as a creature, must necessarily be subject to the laws of his creator, for he is entirely a dependent being. A being, independent of any other, has no rule to pursue, but such as he prescribes to himself; but a state of dependence will inevitably oblige the inferior to take the will of him, on whom he depends, as the rule of his conduct; not indeed in every particular, but in all those points wherein his dependence consists . . .

and consequently as man depends absolutely upon his maker for everything, it is necessary that he should in all points conform to his maker's will."

—William Blackstone, *Commentaries on the Laws of England* (1768)

Millions of Americans falsely believe our *Constitution* requires a separation of church and state; the words are not found in such documents. If there were truly such a wall, explain the following:

- When the federal legislature met in 1789, one of its very first actions was to appoint chaplains in both Houses of Congress.

- Paid chaplains open each session of Congress with a prayer. On the very day Congress approved the wording of the *First Amendment*, its members resolved to request of President Washington a day of public thanksgiving and prayer.

- In 1789, Congress passed the *Northwest Ordinance*, an important document in our history which declared, "Religion, morality, and knowledge, being necessary to good government and the happiness of mankind, schools, and the means of education shall forever be encouraged."

- Every President of the United States (with only one possible exception) has been administered the oath of office with his hand on the Bible, ending with the words, "So help me God."

- The Supreme Court begins every proceeding with the ringing proclamation, "God save the United States and this Honorable Court."

- All currency bears our National Motto,[47] "In God We Trust."[48]

- The Pledge of Allegiance to the Flag affirms that we are "one nation under God." Congress would not allow a comma to be placed after the word *nation*, in order to reflect the basic idea that ours is a "nation founded on a belief in God."

- The *Declaration of Independence* emphatically refers to God.

- The *Declaration of Independence* reads, "All men . . . are endowed by their Creator with certain unalienable Rights, that among these are Life, Liberty, and the Pursuit of Happiness."

- President Abraham Lincoln designated April 30, 1863, as a "national day of prayer and humiliation."

- The *Mayflower Compact* in which our founding fathers invoked the "name of God" to explain why their journey was taken, among other reasons "for the glory of God and advancement of the Christian faith."

- President George Washington proclaimed Thanksgiving, with religious overtones, a day of national celebration and Congress made it a national holiday more than a century ago.[49]

- Many acts of Congress have decreed that federal employees be released from work on religious holidays.

- Art galleries supported by public revenues display religious paintings, inspired by the Christian faith.

- The National Gallery in Washington exhibits masterpieces with religious messages including *The Last Supper, The Birth of Christ, The Crucifixion,* and *The Resurrection,* among many others, with provide explicit Christian themes and messages.[50]

- The chamber of the U.S. Supreme Court is decorated with a notable and permanent symbol of religion, *Moses with the Ten Commandments.*

- Legislative prayers have been upheld by the U.S. Supreme Court.[51]

- The Release Time Program for religious training was approved by the U.S. Supreme Court.[52]

- Sunday closing laws have been upheld by the U.S. Supreme Court.[53]

We cannot afford to retreat from the streets and the halls of government.

- Tax exemptions for church properties was approved by the U.S. Supreme Court.[54]

- Congress approves of federal grants for college buildings of church-sponsored institutions.[55]

- The *Constitution* prohibits any bill to be returned by the President on a Sunday (proof that America was founded as a Christian nation).

- Christmas and Thanksgiving are national holidays.

- "Praise be to God" is engraved on the metal cap of The Washington Monument.

- On tribute walls along the stairway of the Washington Monument, the following are carved:

  In God We Trust
  God in Our Native Land
  Search the Scriptures (John 5:39; Acts 17:11)

  Train up a child in the way he should go and when he is old, he will not depart from it. (Proverbs 22:6)

  Suffer the little children to come unto Me and forbid them not; for such is the kingdom of God. (Luke 18:16)

  May Heaven to this Union continue its beneficence.

- On the rear wall of Washington's tomb is engraved: "I am the Resurrection and the Life; sayeth the Lord. He that believeth in Me, though he were dead yet shall he live. And whosoever liveth and believeth in Me shall never die." (John 11:25–26)

- The Minuteman Statue at Lexington, Massachusetts is in-scribed with words including, "You . . . are placed by Provi-dence in the post of honor, because it is the post of danger . . . let us be [consistent with] nothing unbecoming our characters as Americans, as citizens and Christians, be justly chargeable to us."

If one still believes the lie that there is a total separation of church and state, how can you explain the above facts?

It is wrong for a Christian who lives in America to be ill in-formed of the great issues of the day and uninvolved in providing solutions to the moral challenges we face. It is Christians who must accept blame for allowing our nation to drift so far off the course charted by our founding fathers.

The great attorney Charles Finney, who was converted to Chris-tianity reading biblical references in Blackstone's *Commentaries on the Laws of England*, wrote:

"The church must take right ground in regard to politics . . . the time has come for Christians to vote for honest men, and take consistent ground in politics or the Lord will curse them . . . God cannot sustain this free and blessed country, which we love and pray for, unless the Church will take right ground. Politics are a part of religion in such a country as this, and Christians must do their duty to their country as a part of their duty to God . . . God will bless or curse this nation according to the course Christians take in politics."

Unfortunately, the American dream has become, for many, the American nightmare.

John Adams said:

"Our *Constitution* was made only for a moral and religious people. It is wholly inadequate to the government of any other."

In today's America, the name *Jesus* is not tolerated in many quarters. The sure way to separate the church from the state is to prevent Christians from participating.

God has given American Christians a gracious privilege that few believers in the history of the world have ever known. Millions of Christians around the world risk the loss of their life for being believers in Jesus Christ. They have to pray for freedoms we take for granted everyday.

For their sakes and out of gratitude to our Forefathers and God, we must return to the conflict and engage the enemy. We must stand up, speak up, and refuse to give up, for we do not lose until we quit.

God has given American Christians a gracious privilege that few believers in world history have ever known.

State Constitutions

The belief of importance of God-fearing leaders was so well understood in America that in 1892, the Supreme Court pointed out that of all 44 states then in the Union, each had some type of God-centered declaration in its Constitution.

In reading over the Constitutions of all fifty of our states, I discovered in all fifty, without exception, an appeal or a prayer to the Almighty God of the universe.

As soon as the Founding Fathers returned to their home states, they began to write state constitutions. What did they place in their own constitutions? Thomas McKean and George Read placed in the *Delaware Constitution*:

"Every person, who shall be chosen a member of either House or appointed to any office or placed in trust . . . shall . . . make and subscribe the following declaration, to writ: "I do profess faith in God the Father, and in Jesus Christ, his only Son, and in the Holy Ghost, one God blessed forever more, and I do acknowledge the Holy scriptures of the Old and New Testament given by divine inspiration."[55]

The *Massachusetts Constitution*, authored by Samuel Adams-the Father of the American Revolution-stated:

"We, therefore, the people of Massachusetts, acknowledging, with grateful hearts, the goodness of the great Legislator of the universe, in affording us, in the course of His providence [an opportunity to form a compact]; . . . and devoutly imploring His direction in so interesting a design, . . . [establish this Constitution].

The Governor shall be chosen annually; and no person shall be eligible to this office, unless, at the time of his election . . . he shall declare himself to be of the Christian religion.

Chapter VI, Article I [All persons elected to State office or to the Legislature must] make and subscribe the following declaration, viz. 'I, _____, do declare, that I believe the Christian religion and have firm persuasion of its truth."

The *Preamble* to the *Missouri Constitution* (1875) reads:

"We the people of Missouri, with profound reverence for the Supreme Ruler of the Universe, and grateful for His goodness, do establish this constitution for the better government of the state."

Maryland's new *Constitution* granted complete religious liberty only to the Christians and authorized a general tax "for the support of the Christian religion."[56]

South Carolina's second *Constitution*, adopted in 1778, established the "Christian Protestant Religion" in great detail.[57]

New Hampshire's first *Constitution* did not mention religion, but its *Constitution* in 1784 contained provisions similar to those in the Massachusetts *Constitution*.[58]

Only Protestants could hold public office in New Jersey or sit in the legislatures of Georgia, South Carolina, and New Hampshire, and only those professing the "Christian Religion" could hold public office in Maryland or serve in high government positions in Massachusetts.[59] North Carolina limited public offices to those who believed in God, the truth of the Protestant religion, and the divine authority of both the Old and New Testaments.[60]

Pennsylvania legislators had to declare:

"I do believe in one God, the creator and governor of the universe, the rewarder of the good and the punisher of the wicked. And I do acknowledge the Scriptures of the Old and New Testament to be given by Divine inspiration."[61]

In 1780, in all states except Rhode Island and Connecticut, most of the state constitutions required members of the State Assembly to profess belief in God and the divine inspiration of both the Old and New Testaments.[62]

Should Christians Speak Out?

A most important constitutional right is freedom of speech, which includes the right to speak out on any issue from the biblical perspective. In the ongoing struggle over the direction of our culture, we dare not lose this right. Yet it, along with many of our other freedoms, is under attack. Like everyone else, Christians have the right to be heard. The U.S. Supreme court has continually held that, above all else, the *First Amendment* means that *government has no power to restrict expression because of its message*, ideas, subject matter, or content.

Attempts to stifle Christian voices generally fail the constitutional test. However, all too frequently, Christians back down at even the first hint of oppression. We cannot afford to retreat from the streets and the halls of government. We cannot afford to turn the marketplace of ideas over to those who are ignorant or even hostile to our faith.

We must stop taking our constitutional liberties for granted and take them back. Now, more than ever, we need to not only defend our rights, but to go on the offensive.

We are on the threshold of major change in our country. Our continued and stepped-up involvement is critical to channel the momentum towards true liberty and we must impact our culture for Christ.

In the context of current events today, the issue of church and state rages everywhere as national attention to the problem continually occurs. There are few issues so likely to generate heat rather than light as the question of the proper line between the realm of the state and that of the church.

The seemingly simplicity of the "absolutist" construction of the *First Amendment* is only too patently disingenuous.[63]

Rulings of the United States Supreme Court

"We are a religious people whose institutions presuppose a Supreme Being."

—*Zorach vs. Claussen,*
343 U.S. 313 (1952)

"It has never been thought either possible or desirable to enforce a regimen of total separation . . ."

—*Committee for Public Education
and Religious Liberty vs. Nyquist*
413 U.S. 756 (1973)

"Indeed, we have observed such hostility would bring us into 'war' with our national tradition as embodied in the *First Amendment's* guarantee of the free exercise of religion."

—*Illinois ex rel McCollum vs. Board
of Education,* 333 U.S. 203 (1948)

"This history may help explain why the Court consistently has declined to take a rigid, absolutist view of the Establishment Clause. We have refused "to construe the Religion Clauses with the literalness that would undermine the ultimate constitutional objective as illuminated by history."

—*Walz vs. Tax Commissioner,*
397 U.S. 664 (1970)

"The Constitution [does not] require complete separation of church and state; it affirmatively mandates accommodation, not merely tolerance, of all religions and forbids hostility toward any."

—**Chief Justice Warren Burger**
in *Lynch vs. Donnelly,*
465 U.S. 668 (1984)

"[The] Court has enforced a scrupulous neutrality by the State, as among religions and also as between religions and other activities, but a hermetic separation of the two is an impossibility it has never required."

—*Roemer vs Board of Public Works,*
426 U.S. 736 (1976)

"Devout Christians are destined to be regarded as fools in modern society. We are fools for Christ's sake. We must pray for courage to endure the scorn of the sophisticated world."

—Supreme Court Justice
Antonin Scalia (1999)

"I believe no one can read the history of our country without realizing that the Good Book and the spirit of the Savior have from the beginning been our guiding geniuses. Whether we look to the first Charter of Virginia . . . or to the Charter of New England . . . or the Charter of Massachusetts Bay . . . or to the Fundamental Orders of Connecticut . . . the same objective is present . . . a Christian land governed by Christian principles . . . I like to believe we are living today in the spirit of the Christian religion."

—Supreme Court Justice
Earl Warren[64] (1891–1974)

"Our laws and our institutions must necessarily be based upon the teachings of the Redeemer of Mankind. It is impossible that it should be otherwise; and in this sense and to this extent, our civilization and our institutions are emphatically Christian."

—U.S. Supreme Court, 1982

"God save the United States and this Honorable Court."

—Crier opens each new day
session of the United States
Supreme Court

"Christianity . . . is not to be maliciously and openly reviled and blasphemed against, to the annoyance of believers or to the injury of the public . . . such a case is not to be presumed to exist in a Christian country . . . where can the purest principles of morality be learned so clearly or so perfectly as from the New Testament? It is also said, and truly, that the Christian religion is a part of the common law of Pennsylvania . . ."

—Vidal vs. Girards Executors,
43 U.S. 123 (1844)

"The First Amendment, however, does not say that in every and all respects there shall be a separation of Church and State. That is the common sense of the matter. Otherwise, the state and religion would be aliens to each other—hostile, suspicious, and even unfriendly . . . prayers in our legislative halls, the appeals to the Almighty in the messages of the Chief Executive, the proclamations making Thanksgiving Day a holiday; 'so help me God' in our courtroom oaths—these and all other inferences to the Almighty that run through our laws, our public rituals, our ceremonies would be flouting the First Amendment.

A fastidious atheist or agnostic could even object to the supplication with which the court opens each session: 'God save the United States and this honorable court.'"

—*Zorach vs. Clausen*
343 U.S. 306 (1952)

Writings of United States Presidents

"It is impossible rightly to govern the world without God and the Bible."

—**George Washington**

"Let me live according to those holy rules which Thou hast this day prescribed in Thy Holy Word . . . Direct me to the true object, Jesus Christ the way, the truth, and the life. Bless, O Lord, all the people of this land."

—**George Washington, 1752**

"If we ever forget that we are one Nation under God, then we will be a Nation gone under."

—**Ronald Reagan**

"The basis of our Bill of Rights comes from the teachings we get from Exodus and St. Matthew, from Isaiah and St. Paul. If we don't have a proper fundamental moral background, we will finally end up with a . . . government which does not believe in rights for anybody except the state . . . this is a Christian Nation."

—**Harry S. Truman**

"Taking from the states the moral rule of their citizens, and sub-ordinating it to the general authority (Federal government) would . . . break up the foundations of the Union . . . I believe the States can best govern our home concerns, and the Federal governments our foreign ones."

—Thomas Jefferson

"Fourscore and seven years ago our fathers brought forth on this continent, a new nation, conceived in liberty, and dedicated to the proposition that all men are created equal . . . that this nation, under God, shall have a new birth of freedom and that government of the people, by the people, and for the people, shall not perish from the earth."

—Abraham Lincoln,
November 19, 1863
Gettysburg Address

"America was born a Christian nation. America was born to ex-emplify that devotion to the elements of righteousness which are derived from the revelations of the holy scriptures."

—Woodrow Wilson, May 7, 1911

"It is fit and becoming in all people, at all times, to acknowledge and revere the Supreme Government of God; to bow in humble submission to His chastisement; to confess and deplore their sins and transgressions in the full conviction that the fear of the Lord is the beginning of wisdom; and to pray, with all fervency and contrition, for the pardon of their past offenses, and for a blessing upon their present and prospective action."

—Abraham Lincoln
*Declaring a National Day of Prayer
and Fasting following the Battle of
Bull Run*

"It is the duty of all nations to acknowledge the Providence of Almighty God, to obey His will, to be grateful for His benefits, and to humbly implore His protection and favor."

—George Washington,
October 3, 1789
Proclaiming a National Day of Prayer and Thanksgiving

"God who gave us life gave us liberty. And can the liberties of a nation be thought secure when we have removed their only firm basis, a conviction in the minds of the people that these liberties are a gift of God? That they are not to be violated but with His wrath? Indeed, I tremble for my country when I reflect that God is just; that His justice cannot sleep forever."

—Thomas Jefferson, 1781

"Religion [is] the basis and Foundation of Government."

—James Madison
June 20, 1785

"It is impossible to account for the creation of the universe without the agency of a Supreme Being. It is impossible to govern the universe."

"The belief in a God All Powerful, wise and good, is so essential to the moral order of the World and to the happiness of man, that arguments which enforce it cannot be drawn from too many sources . . ."

—James Madison
November 20, 1785

"The fundamental basis of this Nation's laws was given to Moses on the Mount . . . I don't think we emphasize that enough these days. If we don't have proper fundamental moral background, we will finally end up with a totalitarian government which does not believe in rights for anybody except the state."

—Harry S. Truman
February 15, 1950

"The highest glory of the American Revolution was this, it connected in one dissolvable bond, principles of civil government with the principles of Christianity."

—John Quincy Adams,
July 4, 1821

"The precepts of philosophy . . . laid hold of actions only . . . (but Jesus) pushed His scrutinies into the heart of man, erected His tribunal in the region of the thoughts, and purified the waters at the fountainhead."

—Thomas Jefferson

"We have no government armed with power capable of contending with human passions unbridled by morality and religion . . . our Constitution was made only for a moral and religious people. It is wholly inadequate to the government of any other."

—John Adams[65]

"But we have forgotten God. We have forgotten the gracious Hand which preserved us in peace, and multiplied and enriched and strengthened us; and we have vainly imagined, in the deceitfulness of our hearts, that all these blessings were produced by some superior wisdom and virtue of our own."

—Abraham Lincoln
March 30, 1863

"We have staked the whole future of American civilization, not upon the power of government, far from it. We have staked the future of all our political institutions upon the capacity of mankind for self-government; upon the capacity of each and all of us to govern ourselves, to control ourselves, to sustain ourselves according to *The Ten Commandments of God*."

—James Madison, 1778

"I therefore beg leave to move that henceforth prayers imploring the assistance of Heaven, and its blessing on our deliberations, be held in the Assembly every morning . . . "

—Benjamin Franklin, 1787
Constitutional Convention

Writings of Patriots

"The leaders undertook the voyage 'for the gloree of God, and advancements of the Christian faith and honour of our king and countrie."

—William Bradford, 1620

"What is it that gentlemen wish? What would they have? Is life so dear, or peace so sweet, as to be purchased at the price of chains and slavery? Forbid it, Almighty God! I know not what course others may take; but as for me, give me liberty or give me death!"

—**Patrick Henry**
March 23, 1785

"There is no solid basis for a civilization but in the Word of God. If we abide by the principles taught in the Bible, our country will go on prospering and to prosper. I make it a practice to read the Bible through once every year."

—**Daniel Webster, 1851**

"In this situation of this Assembly, groping as it were in the dark to find political truth, and scarce able to distinguish it when presented to us, how has it happened, Sir, that we have not hitherto once thought of humbly applying to the Father of lights to illuminate our understanding! On the beginning of the Contest with G. Britain, when we were sensible of danger, we had daily prayer in this room for the divine protection—Our prayers, Sir, were heard, and they were graciously answered. All of us who were engaged in the struggle must have observed frequent instances of a superintending providence in our favor. To that kind Providence, we owe this happy opportunity of consulting in peace on the means of establishing our future national felicity. And have we now forgotten this powerful friend? Or do we imagine we no longer need His assistance? I have lived, Sir, a long time, and the longer I live, the more convincing proofs I see of this truth that—God governs in the affairs of men. And if a sparrow cannot fall to the ground without his notice, is it probable that an empire can rise without His aid? We have been assured, Sir, in the Sacred Writings, that 'except the Lord build the House, they labor in vain that build it.' I firmly believe this; and I also believe that without his concurring aid, we shall succeed in this political building no better, than the Builders of Babel: We shall be divided by our little partial local interests; our projects will become confounded and we ourselves shall become a reproach and bye word down to future ages. And what is worse, mankind may hereafter from this unfortunate instance, despair of establishing Governments by Human Wisdom and leave it to chance, war, and conquest."

—**Benjamin Franklin, 1787**
Speech to the Federal Convention

142

"Religion is the only solid basis of good morals: therefore, education should teach the precepts of religion, and the duties of man to God."[73]

—Gouverneur Morris, *First U.S. Minister to France* (1752–1816)

"I am, however, much consoled by reflecting that the religion of Christ has, from its first appearance in the world, been attacked in vain, by all the wits, philosophers, and wise ones, aided by the power of man, and its triumph has been complete . . . I find much cause to reproach myself, that I have lived so long, and have given no decided and public proofs of my being a Christian."

—Patrick Henry, *in a letter to his daughter, Betsy Aylett,* August 20, 1796

"The very existence of the Republic . . . depends much upon the public institutions of religion."

—John Hancock (1737–1793)

"The fundamental objects of the Constitution are in perfect harmony with the revealed objects of the Christian religion. Union, justice, peace, the general welfare, and the blessing of civil and religious liberty, are the objects of Christianity, and always secured under its beneficent reign. The State must rest upon the basis of religion, and it must preserve this basis, or itself must fall . . . this is a Christian Nation, first in name, . . . The chief security and glory of the United States of America has been, is now, and will be forever, the prevalence and domination of the Christian faith."

—Benjamin Morris, (1810–1867) *Historian*

"By our form of government, the Christian religion is the established religion; and all sects and denominations of Christians are placed upon the same equal footing, and are equally entitled to protection in their religious liberty."

—Samuel Chase (1741–1811), *Member, Continental Congress and Associate Supreme Court Justice*

William Patterson, signer of the Constitution, placed on the Supreme Court by George Washington, constantly pointed out that "the Constitution would not keep America on course." He said what would keep America safe would be to obey what God has told us in the sacred scriptures. He would close his speeches with Proverbs 29:2. "When the righteous rule, the people rejoice. When the wicked rule, the people groan."

"Providence has given to our people the choice of their rulers, and it is the duty as well as the privilege and interest of our Christian nation to select and prefer Christians for their rulers."
—John Jay, *First Chief Justice*
of the U.S. Supreme Court
October 12, 1816

". . . we find everywhere a clear recognition of the same truth . . . because of a general recognition of this truth [that we are a Christian nation], the question has seldom been presented to the courts. 'In the Supreme Court's ruling of Updegraph v. The Commonwealth, it was decided that 'Christianity, general Christianity is, and always has been, a part of the common law . . . not Christianity with an established church . . . but Christianity with liberty and conscience to all men.'"
—David Josiah Brewer, (1892)
Justice of the U.S. Supreme Court
Quoting the charters of Virginia,
the pilgrims in the Mayflower Compact,
the Fundamental Orders of Connecticut,
the Charter of Privileges granted to the Province of
Pennsylvania, and the Declaration of Independence

"The people of this State, in common with the people of this country, profess the general doctrines of Christianity, as the rule of their faith and practice. . . . We are a Christian people, and the morality of the country is deeply engrafted upon Christianity, and not upon the doctrines or worship of those imposters [other religions] . . . It is also said, and truly, that the Christian religion is a part of the common law . . . proven by the volume of unofficial declarations to the mass of utterances that this is a Christian nation. We find everywhere a clear recognition of this same truth."

—James Kent (1763–1847)
Chief Justice, Supreme
Court of New York

"The great pillars of all government and of social life . . . [are] virtue, morality, and religion. This is the armor, my friend, and this alone, renders us invincible."

—Patrick Henry (1736–1799)

"One of the beautiful boasts of our municipal jurisprudence is that Christianity is a part of the Common Law . . . There never has been a period in which the Common Law did not recognize Christianity as lying at its foundations . . . I verily believe Christianity necessary to the support of civil society."

—Joseph Storey
Father of American Jurisprudence

"[N]ational prosperity can neither be obtained nor preserved without the favor of Providence."

—John Jay (1817–1894)

"[T]he most important of all lessons [from the Scriptures] is the denunciation of ruin to every State that rejects the precepts of religion."

—Gouverneur Morris (1752–1816)
Penman and Signer
of the Constitution

The Decline of Judeo-Christian Morality

"Righteousness exalts a nation, but sin is a reproach to any nation."
—Proverbs 14:34

"God will keep His covenant with His people, if His people obey the divine commands."

The multicultural attack on biblical morality and values is an assault on America's moral infrastructure. Once our system of morality with its age-old proven results crumbles, then our nation is doomed. Our system is undergirded by freedoms, rights, and economic opportunities. We should ask a simple question, "Show us another system of morality equal to the Judeo-Christian morality that has served a nation better." There is none.

Our norms and values come from God whom we have honored by inscribing His name on coins, public buildings, The Pledge of Allegiance, and patriotic songs. Today, however, there are numerous pro-abortion, pro-homosexual, and pro-lesbian groups, as well as pedophilic organizations, which are given widespread public forums and promotions.

If this behavior is legitimized, it violates the natural and moral law and the destruction of America's soul is inevitable. With regard to America's moral decline as a result of sexual promiscuity, Dr. Paul Cameron says:

> "At no time in history has a society departed so quickly and so radically from traditional norms, and at no time in history has such conduct been so dangerous."

Those who would warn the United States about its deteriorating morality are called narrow-minded, bigoted, or homophobic. The homophobic label is often erroneously pinned on anyone who opposes homosexuality and to intimidate those who see homosexual behavior as morally wrong. The "anointed" often use this term as a way of "avoiding substantive debate."[73]

America must not let itself be fooled into believing multiculturalism's message that there is no absolute code of right or wrong, and that all morality is culturally relative. This "values clarification" now used in many public schools may sound good but teaches students that there is no right or wrong. Merely being asked to express their "values," feelings, ideas, and beliefs in terms of their own subjective value system is wrong. Those who express their values in the terms of the Ten Commandments or the Judeo-Christian ethic frequently are seen as "out of step" and ridiculed.

The multicultural values clarification (multi-morality) is wrong and dangerous. If it teaches that any behavior is acceptable so long as there is some group or subcultural support, then no culture's behavior may be criticized, much less penalized. The end result of such a system is moral anarchy.[74]

As America fights multiculturalism and remembers its past victories, we must be willing to fear and respect God's moral law. This message is not new. The United States heard it a century ago from Katherine Lee Bates, writer of America the Beautiful, who pointedly told the nation:

> "America! America! God mend thine eve'ry flaw,
> Confirm Thy soul in self-control, Thy liberty in law."

"**The time for excuses is over.** The returns are in on the brave new world of liberal social policy, and they are not good. We now know that the left is peddling from an empty wagon.

The American people face a great and important political task—to reassert their influence on the social institutions—and win the battle for the culture. Whoever wins the battle for the culture gets to teach the children.

So be it. Reclaiming our institutions is less a political opportunity than a civic obligation. It involves hard work. But it is work of imminent importance. At the end of the day, somebody's values will prevail. This is what a democracy—a government of, by, and for the people—is all about. The debate has been joined. But the fight for our values has just begun."[1]

> My eager desire and hope being that I may never fall ashamed, but that now as ever I may do honor to Christ in my own person by fearless courage.
> **—Phillipians 1:20**

1. Bennett, William J., *The Devaluing of America* (Colorado Springs, CO: Focus on the Family, 1992), 266–267.

Kathy Willens/AP Photo

Father Brian Jordan (second from left) returned to Ground Zero on October 4. The friend of the late Father Mychal Judge blessed the cross of steel beams that had been found amidst the rubble of Tower No. 1.

OUR FUTURE

❖

America began with a dream, a dream shaped by Christianity. This dream, the American dream, is what has made the rest of the world look to America in hope. The basic concepts of America are undergirded by traditional religion.

We have separated the church from the state to protect private religious faith from government interference. We do not want our government explicitly embracing a particular religion that will coerce religious practice. Some separation of church and state is a valuable tool for preserving the religious liberty of people.

However, to confuse the desire of the Framers to prohibit the establishment of a national church as opposed to discrimination against religious sects by building an impenetrable wall between religious faith and political action is wrong.

All citizens, religious or not, are the "bearers of opinion," and it is from their opinions that government policy is derived in our democracy. The importance of the interaction between religious faith and political action cannot be overstated.

Christians should take advantage of the opportunity available to them to participate in the process, to actualize their faith through social institutions.

"Our Constitution was made only for a moral and religious people. It is wholly inadequate to the government of any other."
—John Adams
(1735–1826)
Second President
of the U.S.

"The character of a society is determined by how well it transmits true and time honored values from generation to generation."
—William J. Bennett
Former Secretary
of Education

Christians have been said to ". . . tolerate even the worst, and if need be, the most atrocious form of government."[1]

The example of Christ's submission to Pilate and explicit teachings of Paul regarding submission to government authorities is powerful evidence in favor of a pietism which rejects efforts to affect culture. There is no biblical justification for placing limits upon the sovereignty of God. By shrinking God to fit the narrow confines of inward faith and formalized worship, Christians ignore the clear implications of the teachings of Jesus Christ.

Those who would divorce their religious faith from any outward actions have no standing to complain about the deteriorating moral fabric of American culture. In any successful political system, stability and coherence are fundamental. People want a government capable of "reliable behavior on fixed principles persisting through changed situations."[2]

People of faith have been lured into a state of mind where we're content to sit back and leave it to someone else.

But fixed principles must come from somewhere. If the people themselves have no common set of values, it is meaningless to ask the government to obtain its guiding principles from a barren field. Absent the participation of those who adhere to moral absolutes, the destabilizing forces of relativism carry the day by default.

In his *Memorial and Remonstrance*, James Madison wrote:

"Much more must every man who becomes a member of any particular civil society, do it with a saving of his allegiance to the Universal Sovereign."

The critic who claims, "You can't legislate morality" misses the point. In reality, governments legislate almost nothing but morality. Virtually every government action, from determining the proper level at which to set tax rates to deciding whether abortion should be legal, involves some moral choice. A government powerless to regulate moral behavior is a government powerless to govern.

Silence in the face of evil is morally culpable behavior. Whether the failure of Christians to affect society is the result of benign neglect or moral cowardice, the results are unacceptable. Our Bible must never be reduced to a play book for social activism. Christians are not free to abandon the social implications of their faith and then gasp in amazement at the ugliness of the cultural collapse.

Should religion become "privatized" and cease to affect public life? Christians, if they do not speak and act effectively on their faith, will have very little impact on the culture that surrounds them. Christ taught that the norm for the true Christian is the exertion of some moral influence on society. This is defined as "salt" to the culture:

> "You are the salt of the earth. But if the salt has become tasteless, how will it be made salty again?"
>
> —Matthew 5:13

As an early theologian, Jay Gresham Machen, pointed out one hundred years ago:

> "We may preach with all the fervor of a reformer and yet succeed only in winning a straggler here and there, if we permit the whole collective thought of the nation . . . to be controlled by ideas which, by the restless force of logic, prevent Christianity from being regarded as anything more than a harmless delusion."

America's Spiritual Roots

When the early pioneers landed on the shores of America, they brought with them a vision. Though certainly not all were Chris-

tian, a large portion of the pioneers operated under a Judeo-Christian world view. They believed their history had a purpose and in a real sense these pioneers were missionaries to America bringing the Gospel of Jesus Christ.

When they landed, they erected crosses. They framed their colonial documents and expressed their views as to their purpose in life to spread the Gospel. They stated laws should be consistent with the Bible and in reality derived their laws from the Bible. In creating the federal government, the founders drew from the source that if God did not build this house of America, those who labored did so in vain.

Even the average student who did not claim to be a Christian probably knew more about the Bible than many of today's young people who regularly attend church. Many of the Founders knew the original languages of the Bible and it was not unusual for them to study Greek and Latin. Today, a large number of our students graduate from public schools and do not even understand English.

There is a struggle going on today for the heart and soul of America. This struggle involves the Judeo-Christian heritage of this country and religious freedom.

> "In the same way, let your light shine before men, that they may see your good deeds and praise your Father in heaven."
> —**Matthew 5:16** (NIV)

Religion has a vital role to play in the political life of America and Christians should ask, "How then should I live?" The answer is, Christians must run for office, support candidates of their choice, attend school board meetings, and become actively involved in the political process at all levels.

The lure of Washington is strong and it is tempting to look toward that city as the focal point for political action. But for most people, it will be at the state and local levels where the greatest impact is made. For example, supporting candidates for the school board can greatly affect our local communities.

Political courage is a rare commodity but those who possess it can quickly step into positions of influence. State and local party organizations, local candidates, and lobbying organizations are all constantly in search of leaders. There is never a shortage of work to be done. All that is required is a willingness to get involved and to do the job with excellence. Christians have an obligation to be good citizens and that includes more than just obeying laws and voting. It means actively participating in the political process.

LaSalle Erecting a Cross

The decision to remain on the sidelines of society is a decision to abandon culture to the savageness of human life absent God. Good citizens cannot be content to watch their nation and their fellow citizens suffer such a fate. Christians can change public policy, and they should work energetically to use their status as citizens to open up opportunities for the advancement of Christian principles within the political system.

We are blessed by God to be Christians *and* Americans, but there are many of us who have well forgotten exactly what God's blessing on America means. We have been lured into a state of mind where we're content to sit back and leave it to someone else.[3] In this land, there is no conflict between citizenship and faith. The greatest test of faith is to bring that faith to life in citizenship.

There are many who argue Christians should avoid involvement in government, law and politics. Christians who interact in political affairs are routinely admonished, "That preacher needs to get back into the pulpit and get his nose out of politics."

A growing bureaucratic federal government is not compatible with freedom, particularly religious freedom. As bureaucracy grows, the trend towards secularism and political correctness continues to mount. There is an increasing clash between a secularistic mindset and Judeo-Christian world views. As secularism triumphs, the god of the state eats away the religious symbols of yesteryear.

The symbols of our Fathers are being removed one-by-one according to Matthew D. Staver in *Faith and Freedom*:

- For many years the city of St. Cloud, Florida, erected a cross atop its water tower. After a lawsuit, the cross is now gone.
- Corpus Christi, a city whose name means "The Body of Christ," had for decades erected crosses to commemorate Easter and the resurrection of Jesus Christ. Now city officials removed them out of fear of litigation.
- A Michigan school had a painting of Jesus hanging in the hallway. The painting was donated to the school and had been displayed for many years. One parent objected and the painting is now gone.
- Rolling Meadows, Illinois, had a cross in one of the quadrants of its city seal. Now the cross is gone and the seal is changed.
- Republic, Missouri, had an ichthus or "sign of the fish" in one of four quadrants of its city seal. The city was settled by Christians, and its earliest buildings were Christian churches. A lawsuit was filed by a local Wiccan. The quadrant is now vacant.
- Most public schools began each day with prayer. Now all public schools are forbidden to begin with a morning prayer.
- Most public schools sang religious Christmas carols. Now, most prohibit the singing of Christmas carols.
- "The world needs God" was removed from an Illinois courthouse.
- Stowe, Ohio, was required to remove the cross from its official seal after being sued by the ACLU.

- "With God all things are possible" was removed by the State of Ohio.
- A first grade student at Haines School in Medford, New Jersey, was not allowed to tell a story about "Jacob and Esau" at story time.
- A recent federal court case disallowed a public cemetery to have a planter in the shape of a cross. The court explained that if someone were to view the cross, it could cause "emotional distress."[4]
- A federal court recently ruled a school teacher could not be seen publically with his own personal copy of the Bible and ordered that a classroom library with nearly 250 books remove the two books which dealt with Christianity.[5]
- A man was convicted of brutally murdering and clubbing to death a 71-year old woman with an axe handle to steal her Social Security check. The jury's conviction was overturned because the prosecuting attorney, in closing argument, mentioned a Bible verse in the courtroom.[6]

When Alexis de Tocqueville traveled this country in the 1830's, he stated:

"The religious aspect of the country was the first thing that struck my attention."[7]

If Alexis de Tocqueville returned to America today in the 21st century, I wonder what would impress him now? If he visited our public schools, would he be impressed by the religious influence? When the class began, would he hear a prayer? Would he look at the instructional book and see religious influences? When he talked to our representative leadership on the state or federal level, would he be impressed by their desire to serve this country out of a sense of mission?

Or, instead, would he be impressed with the rising tide of teen-age pregnancy, drugs, suicide, abortion, crime and indiscriminate mass shootings? Would he feel safe when he entered our nation's capitol, one of the leading crime areas of the world? Would he be impressed with the way we have erased most of our religious heritage from public life?

The issue of religious freedom in the public square is a battle for the heart and soul of America. If we lose religious freedom in the public square, then we have lost America forever. As religion goes, so goes America. The early founders knew the importance of religion and were willing to forsake their homes, comfort, families, and even sacrifice their lives for freedom.

Today we have grown complacent—if we do not catch the vision that they once held—if we let the flame of freedom that they carried die out, then this country, as we know it, will come to an end. Like an avalanche of snow tumbling down a mountain, it will crumble as surely as other world governments have crumbled in past decades.[8]

The real history of the founding of this nation does not lie. Our forefathers, almost to the person, believed in God. They were students of the Old and New Testaments and deeply influenced by the life and teachings of Jesus. They founded our nation on principles basic to our Judeo-Christian heritage. They feared for the future of this nation if the people ever turned from those principles.[9]

But the feared day has come. Our nation's spiritual heritage is being systematically eliminated from historical record.

A whole generation of American students are being cheated out of an honest, thorough, uncensored look at our nation's past. Public and private lives are being transformed by it.

We must look at the exciting days in early American history when our forefathers clearly demonstrated the early spiritual directions of this nation.

The Culture War

Where do Christians stand in the culture war? Some conclude that Americans no longer care about right and wrong and feel believers should throw up their hands and surrender. Should we continue to defend the unborn child, oppose the homosexual agenda, fight for lower taxes, promote pro-family initiatives in Congress, and continue to defend the family and Judeo-Christian values? Has the Christian community given up on the effort to influence our representative form of government?

Some are afraid that it is patently illegal for churches to become involved in campaigns and elections and the IRS will revoke the tax-exempt status of organizations that violate the law. There has only been one church in recent memory that has suffered this fate.[10]

The political system does not belong exclusively to those with whom we disagree, and we should not yield a single victory to them without fighting for what we believe! This is the way a democracy works. It is a representative form of government that should involve every citizen. It was designed, as Lincoln said, ". . . of the people, by the people, and for the people."[11] This includes people of faith and it is foolish to assume that once a person becomes a believer in Jesus Christ he should be disenfranchised and silenced.

What's at stake in our history is profoundly more significant than the whims of politics. Hanging in the balance is the essence of Christian faith: purity, reverence for life, family stability, love for God, and reception to the Gospel itself.[12]

Political correctness has institutionalized censorship of speech and the very formation of ideas. The American family is under siege by state agencies and our culture at large. But governmental institutions from the Supreme Court and President to the Legislature are not solely to blame. Past generations of Christians and other religionists who did not become involved in society and who watched silently as the culture shifted towards the secular world view are also responsible.

It is a mistake as a matter of history, to assert that religion clauses command "mutual abstention—keeping politics out of religion and religion out of politics."[13]

*Abraham Lincoln
(1809–1865)*

From politically active ministers such as Samuel Davies and John Witherspoon, to Reinhold Niebuhr and Martin Luther King, Jr., in modern times, American history is replete with examples of religious leaders entering the political arena and influencing social policy.[14]

The participation of religious groups in public issues such as the abolition of slavery, school prayer, civil rights, the reduction of nuclear arms, and opposition to homosexuality and abortion, is evidence of a free society.

The U.S. Supreme Court, which sustained New York's tax exemption for churches, properly noted:

> "Of course, churches as much as secular bodies and private citizens have the right to speak to public issues. No perfect or absolute separation is really possible; the very existence of the religion clauses is an involvement of sorts—one that seeks to mark boundaries to avoid excessive entanglement."[15]

Having affirmed the right to speak on public issues, merely because one has the right to speak, does not mean it is always prudent to do so. When religious leaders enter the political arena, they expose themselves to competing views and often harsh rhetoric and risk losing sight of their spiritual calling.[16] The solution most consistent with our historical commitment to religious liberty and free speech should be to welcome religious expression.

Former Secretary of Education William J. Bennett put it best:

Pulpit in Revolution

"During the last three decades a lot has gone wrong in America. Our society is far more violent and vulgar than it used to be. We have experienced enormous increases in violent crime, out of wedlock births, abortions, divorces, suicides, child abuse, and welfare dependancy. The answer to much of what ails us is spiritual and moral regeneration. Yet some liberals would have us believe that the greatest threat to our Republic are people with strong religious convictions who are actively involved in politics. This is nonsense . . . the attempt to discredit the conservative Christian movement is an attempt by some to discredit its underlying philosophy . . . Christianity is about right and wrong. And politics is, too."[17]

Those who would cordon off religious thought from our nation's political discourse are adopting a position wholly contrary to both America's history and its ideals.

Political Correctness

Unfortunately, some have sought to redefine America and have won the battle of words. They call wrong right, and evil good, and they have confused countless millions as a result.

Verbal Engineering. Words are very powerful tools. The Apostle James reminded us:

"If anyone considers himself religious and yet does not keep a tight rein on his tongue, he deceives himself and his religion is worthless. . . . Consider what a great forest is set on fire by a small spark. The tongue also is a fire, a world of evil . . ."
—**James 1:26; 3:5b**

Some things do not change. Words have been used as powerful weapons throughout human history, sometimes for good and sometimes for bad.

For example, a short time ago the word *abortion* clearly meant the killing of an unborn child. Now we say *reproductive rights* or *reproductive liberty*. A divorce now means *dissolution of marriage*. Welfare means *public assistance*. Homosexuality is now labeled as an *alternative lifestyle* and has been given a legal, protected, and elevated platform as a new *civil right*.

Legal Engineering. Through strategic use and abuse of the court system, engineers have turned wrongs into rights through litigation.

The current philosophy of "political correctness" holds that certain ideas are automatically taboo and that Christians should not seek to persuade others to their religious beliefs. This had led to a consensus within society that anything is acceptable. Nothing is right or wrong; it is only a matter of preference.

Modern secular societies have accepted relativism as a basis for their social norms. This means that absolutes are debunked. But in the Great Commission, Christ charged Christians to philosophically challenge belief systems.[18]

America's Secularization

The old absolute rule was:

Religion is the backbone of American culture, providing the moral and spiritual light needed for public and private life.

The new enlightened thinking is:

"Religion is the bane of public life, so for the public good it should be banned from the public square."

The demise of religion has been the subject of many best selling books wherein many persons encourage a tendency to say of religious belief: "Yes, we cherish you—now go away and leave us alone."[19]

We are told religion is like building model airplanes, just another hobby: something quiet, something private, something trivial—not really fit activity for intelligent, public-spirited adults.[20]

The term "religious cleansing" best describes the current hostility and bigotry toward religion and people of faith. Christian views on contemporary major issues are seen as "religious" and religious views are to be kept in church buildings or behind the front doors of our homes lest we somehow violate contemporary notions of the separation of church and state. If we move into the city halls, courts, public schools, or federal offices, then we become trespassers; violators who need to be pushed back to the private sphere where our ideas cannot impact anyone but ourselves.[21]

Believers of all faiths face an increasingly hostile culture in which religion can play only a private role such as a hobby. Those who practice it are generally caricatured as extremists, fundamentalists, religious zealots, and right-wing fanatics. "Keep your faith at home."

Strategy of Secularists

"In an order to ensure to citizens freedom of conscience, the church in the U.S.S.R. is separated from the State, and the school from the church."

—Article 124
Constitution of the United Soviet
Socialist Republic (1922–1991)

There are specific mechanisms to complete the task of immobilizing and silencing conservative Christians:

1. Deny our Judeo-Christian roots and rewrite our historical records.

2. Convince American people that Christians, specifically those with conservative inclinations, are in violation of the *Constitution* whenever they advocate their views beyond the front doors of their sanctuaries.

3. Embarrass, insult, shout down, and mischaracterize the conservative Christians, hoping to intimidate them into silence. The names "radical right," "far right," "extreme right," "bigot," "hate speech," or "fundamentalist" are part of the effort to marginalize those with traditional views.

We are witnesses to an unprecedented campaign to secularize our society and demoralize our institutions from the top down. This effort has been enormously successful. The predictable is happening—a generation of young people growing up with little understanding of the spiritual principles upon which our country was founded. We have taught them that right and wrong are arbitrary—subjective—changing. They have learned their lessons well.

We live in a culture that is morally indifferent.

We see America sinking into a morass of cultural depravity and ultimately our political decline at the end of the day. There is a fierce secularism relentlessly penetrating our defenses - the spectacle of a mighty nation committing a slow suicide.[22] We worry about America's continued viability and wonder - is it too late? Is America just another piece of real estate, no different than any other country? It is late, but not too late. There is a road back.

The Washington Post reported February 1, 1993, that members of the Christian Right were, ". . . largely poor, uneducated, and easy to command."[23]

We must restore the values that have molded our national character. These values have come under an across-the-board assault. They continue to be ridiculed and mocked today.

America is a God-fearing nation and we must proceed from that basic premise. This country was literally founded on faith in God.

Ninety percent of Americans believe in God. Nearly 100 percent of the Congress of the United States does as well. We are a nation of believers and most of us read, study, and try to conform our lives to the teaching of the Bible. It is time to end the scoffing at religion, especially at Christianity, that goes on among the self-anointed elites in the media, entertainment industry and academia.

A restoration of values means understanding that there are some universal truths–some constants. Each person does not have the right to invent a value system and pass it off as good for the rest of society.

James Madison, the primary drafter of the Constitution, summed it up perfectly:

> "We have staked the future of all of our political institutions upon the capacity of each and all of us to control ourselves, to sustain ourselves according to the Ten Commandments."

The Cultural Dividing Line

> "People armed in the holy cause of liberty, and in such a country as that which we possess are invincible by any force which our enemy can send against us . . . [we] shall not fight our battles alone . . .

There is a just God who presides over the destinies of nations, and who will rise up friends to fight our battles for us."
—**Patrick Henry**

Religion seems to be a cultural dividing line. The left, liberal elite despise traditional religious beliefs, although they may be sympathetic to the liberal National Council of Churches. Liberals are profoundly uncomfortable with religious institutions and the traditional values they embody.

The liberal media uses the words *fundamentalist, born again,* or most horribly *the religious right.* In their minds, these words put an end to any argument, guaranteed to call forth not simply criticism, but also ridicule and an attitude of intellectual superiority. Thus, anyone who might take the religious right seriously on anything automatically forfeits his intellectual respectability.

How Shall We Live?

"Now more than ever before, the people are responsible for the character of their Congress. If that body be ignorant, reckless and corrupt, it is because the people tolerate ignorance, recklessness, and corruption. If it be intelligent, brave, and pure, it is because the people demand these high qualities to represent them in the national legislature . . . if the next centennial does not find us a great nation . . . it will be because those who represent the enterprise, the culture, and the morality of the nation do not aid in controlling the political forces."
—**James A. Garfield (1831–1881)**
A Century of Congress
July 1876

Centuries ago when the Jews were in exile, they cried out to God, "How should we then live?"[24] Today the same question should be asked. "How shall we live today?"

After 2000 years, in this extraordinary moment for the Christian church, the birth of the Son of God still remains the defining moment of history.

Jesus founded a church that could not be destroyed, and hundreds of millions of followers affirm Jesus as the same yesterday, today, and forever.

But many Christians feel that they are experiencing some of the same sense of exile that Jews did in the time of Ezekiel. We live in a culture that is morally indifferent.

Judeo-Christian values are mocked and immorality in high places is not only ignored but sometimes rewarded. Disintegrating personal behavior is endangering the life of our nation.

When Christians make good faith efforts to halt this slide, they are maligned as intolerant or bigoted. Many people have concluded that the "culture war" is over. Battle weary, Christians retreat into the safety of their own sanctuaries by keeping busy and plugging into band-aid social programs offered, hoping to keep themselves and their children safe from the coming desolation.[25]

Christians see a biblical mandate, God's sovereignty over all of life. Turning their backs on this culture is a betrayal of this mandate. Americans are groping for something that will restore the shattered bonds of family and community, something that will make sense out of life.

Christianity offers a way to understand both the physical and the moral order—a comprehensive world-wide view that covers all areas of life and thought. Only Christianity offers a way to live in line with the real world. Our forefathers knew the Christian world view was a consistent, rational and workable belief system.

What then is the answer that God gave His people when they cried out, "How should we then live?" Through the prophet Ezekiel, God admonished the people to repent—to turn from their evil ways and turn toward Him—and to show their neighbors that their hope is in His justice and righteousness.

God's word to us today is precisely the same. In a 1950 Nobel Peace Prize acceptance speech, William Faulkner declared:

> "I decline to accept the end of man. Man will not merely endure but prevail because he alone among creatures has a soul, a spirit capable of compassion, and sacrifice, and endurance."

Today in America, we must in the same way decline to accept the end of moral man. We must carry on the struggle for our children, and we must push back hard against an age that is pushing very hard against us. And when we do, we will emerge victorious against the trials of our time. And when we do, we will save our children from the decadence of our time. And when we do, then we will be able to sing confidently again about the country we love and those beautiful words of old:

> *"Oh beautiful for heroes proved in liberating strife,*
> *Who more than self their country loved,*
> *And mercy more than life!*
> *America! America! May God thy gold refine.*
> *'Til all success be nobleness,*
> *And every gain divine."*[26]

"We Hold These Truths . . ."

America has been a blessing to our Forefathers and to us, and will be a blessing to future generations if we keep faith with the founding vision.

The great threat to the American experiment today is not from enemies abroad, but from within. That disorder is increasingly expressed in a denial of the very concept of moral truth which is now painfully familiar. Abortion, crime, drug abuse, family disintegration, teenage suicide, pornography—all are rampant in our society.

People who are motivated by religion or religiously-inspired morality are relegated to a category of second-class citizenship. Increasingly, law and public policy are pitted against the social and moral convictions of the people, with the result that millions of Americans feel alienated from a government that they no longer recognize as their own.

We will be judged by history and by our God—not according to the political victories we achieve. We must remain faithful to a calling that is uniquely ours—speak the truth, in season and out of season, no matter how unpopular, and always in love.

Old fashioned values still have relevance today. As Ted Koppel of ABC's *Nightline* once observed, they are the Ten Commandments; "not the Ten Suggestions."

What America needs is not political revolution, but spiritual renewal. We must realize how little government and politics can accomplish. If people of faith pour all of their dreams into political activity, they will be sorely disappointed. We cannot identify our religious convictions with the platform of a particular political party.

All Americans must be urged to work together to create what Pope John Paul, II, called a "culture of life." God's motives are higher than ours, and His message of love and redemption transcends politics.

What does it mean for a person of faith to be involved in politics and government? It is no different from being a Christian in any other vocation.[27] We are people of faith struggling to do what is right, nothing more. We are sometimes wrong, but as Abraham Lincoln observed during the Civil War:

> "While I know that God is always on the side of the right and that He hates injustice, I am less concerned about whether God is on our side than I am that we be found on His."

Such is the experiment in ordered liberty that has been entrusted to our hands.

"Hear ye, Hear ye, Hear ye,
United States District Court is now in session.
God save the United States and this honorable court"
Official opening of all federal courts.

Our Past
NOTES

1. Flexner, James Thomas, George Washington and the American Revolution, (Boston: Little, Brown, 1967), 76; Flexner, James Thomas, "Providence Rides the Storm," American Heritage, (Dec. 1967), 13–17, pp. 98–99.
2. Marshall, Peter and Manuel, David, The Light and the Glory, (Old Tappan, NJ: Fleming H. Revel Co., 1940), p. 318.
3. Bancroft, George, History of the United States of America. (Boston: Little, Brown, 1879, 3:72.
4. Schmidt, Alvin J., The Menace of Multiculturalism: Trojan Horse in America, (Westport, CT: Praeger Publishers, 1997), p. 178.
5. von Kuehnelt-Leddihn, Erik, Leftism Revisited: From Sade and Marx to Hitler and Polpot, (Washington, DC: Regnery Gateway, 1990), p. 67.
6. Washington, H.A., Works, Thomas Jefferson, (New York: Derby and Jackson, 1859), 2:332.
7. Rush, Benjamin, A Plan for the Establishment of Public Schools, (Philadelphia: 1786), reprinted in Essays on Education in the Early Republic by Frederick Rudolph (Cambridge, MA: The Beknap Press of Harvard University Press, 1965), p. 10.
8. Although there exists no contemporary portrait of Christopher Columbus, we are fortunate to have descriptions of his appearance, personality, and character from men who knew him including his son, Ferdinand.
9. Morrison, Samuel Eliot., *The Oxford History of the American People.* (Oxford University Press: New York, 1965), p. 25.
10. Noll, Mark A., *A History of Christianity in the United States and Canada.* (Grand Rapids, MI: William Eerdmans Publishing Co., 1992), p. 12.
11. Federer, William J., *America's God and Country, Encyclopedia of Quotations.* (Coppell, TX: Fame Publishing, Inc.), pp. 113–114.
12. Morrison, Samuel Eliot., *The European Discovery of America.* (New York: Oxford University Press, 1974), pp. 58–60.
13. Ibid, p. 141.
14. Federer, William J., *America's God and Country Encyclopedia of Quotations.* (Coppell, Texas: Fame Publishing, Inc.), pp. 435–436.
15. Morrison, Samuel Eliot., *The Oxford History of the American People.* (Oxford University Press: New York, 1965), p. 26.

16. Lutz, Donald S., *The Origins of American Constitutionalism: The Colonial Heritage, Juris* (Christian Legal Society: 1987), p. 8.
17. Bradford, William. Of Plymouth Plantation, Commonwealth of Massachusetts Edition. (Boston: Wright and Porter, 1989); Bradford, William, Of Plymouth Plantation: 1606–1646, edited by W.T. Davis (New York: Charles Scribner and Sons, 1908); Bradford, William, Of Plymouth Plantation, 1620–1647, Edited by Samuele Morrison, Alfred A. Knopf, (New York, 1952).
18. White-Notson, Adelia and Robert Carver, Stepping Stones: The Pilgrims Own Story, (Portland, OR: Binford and Mort Publishing, 1987), p. 191.
19. Ibid, p. 194.
20. Davis, W.T. Of Plymouth Plantation, William Bradford, (New York: Charles Scribner and Sons, 1908).
21. Adair, John, Founding Fathers: The Puritans in England and America, (London: J.M. Dent and Sons, Ltd., 1982), p. 122.
22. Ibid, p. 123–126.
23. Adair, John, Founding Fathers: The Puritans in England and America, (London: J.M. Dent and Sons, Ltd., 1982).
24. Ibid, p. 2.
25. Ibid, p. 9.
26. Ibid, 265–266.
27. *The Basic Symbols of the American Political Tradition* (Baton Rouge, LA: Kendall and Carey: LSU Press, 1970).
28. Levy, Leonard W., *America: A Narrative History.* (New York, NY: W.W. Norton and Co., 1984) p. 35.
29. Boorstin, Daniel J., *The Americans: The Colonial Experience.* (New York: Vintage Books, 1958), p. 3.
30. Noll, Mark A., *A History of Christianity in the United States and Canada.* (Grand Rapids, MI: William Eerdmans Publishing Co., 1992), p. 33.
31. Linder, Robert D., A Civil Religion and Historical Perspective: The Reality that Underlies the Concept, *Journal of Church and State 17,* (Autumn 1775), p. 405.
32. Miller, Robert T. and Flowers, Ronald B., *Toward Benevolent Neutrality: Church, State, and the Supreme Court* (Waco, TX: Markham Press Fund, 1977), p. 563.
33. Lutz, Donald S., The Relative Influence of European Writers on Late Eighteenth Century American Political Thought, *American Political Science Review,* 189 (1984), pp. 195–196.

34. Eidsmoe, John, *Christianity and the Constitution*. (Grand Rapids, MI: Baker Books, 1987), p. 58.

35. Federer, William J., *America's God and Country Encyclopedia of Quotations* (Coppell, TX: Fame Publishing, Inc., 1994), pp. 427–428.

36. Sandburg, Carl, An Interview with Frederick Van Ryn, *This Week Magazine*, January 4, 1953, p. 11.

37. Sandburg, Carl, *Remembrance Rock*, Epilogue, Ch. 2, 1001 (1948).

38. President Abraham Lincoln in a proclamation appointing a National Fast Day, March 30, 1863. Basler, Roy. *The Collected Works of Abraham*, (1953), Vol. 6, 156.

39. Storey, Joseph, *Storey's Commentaries on the Constitution of the United States*, Vol. II, Boston: Hilliard, Gray and Co., 1833 (Fifth Ed. 1981), pp. 630–631.

40. Noll, Mark A., *A History of Christianity in the United States and Canada*. (Grand Rapids, MI: William Eerdmans Publishing Co., 1992), p. 147.

41. Federer, William J., America's God and Country Encyclopedia of Quotations (Coppell, TX: Fame Publishing, Inc., 1994) p. 12.

42. Fletcher v Peck, 6 Cranch 87 (1799).

43. *Thomas Jefferson, The Writings of Thomas Jefferson* (Washington, D.C.: The Thomas Jefferson Memorial Association, 1904), Vol. XII, p. 292.

44. Bergh, Albert Ellery, *The Writings of Thomas Jefferson* (Washington, D.C.: The Thomas Jefferson Memorial Association, 1904), Vol. XVI, 281–282, letter to Danbury Baptist Association, January 1, 1802; Barton, David, *The Myth of Separation* (Aldeo, TX: Wall Builder Press, 1991).

45. Everson vs. Board of Education, 330 U.S. 1 (1947).

46. Eidsmoe, John, *Christianity and the Constitution* (Grand Rapids, Baker Books, 1987), p. 360.

47. Manuel, David and Marshall, Peter, *In God They Trusted* (Pittsburgh: Crossroads Christian Communications, 1983), p. 45.

48. Garrity, Patrick J., *A Sacred Union of Citizens*. (London: Roman and Littlefield Publishers, 1996), p. 2.

49. Fitzpatrick, John C., First Inaugural Address, April 30, 1789, *The Writings of George Washington from the Original Manuscript Sources, 1745–1799*, 30:394; Farewell Address, Paragraph 27 (Washington: U.S. Government Printing Office, 1931–1944).

50. Garrity, Patrick J., *A Sacred Union of Citizens.* (London: Roman and Littlefield Publishers, 1996), p. 6.

51. Fitzpatrick, John C., Washington to George Steptoe Washington, March 23, 1789, *The Writings of George Washington from the Original Manuscript Sources, 1745–1799*, 30:248 (Washington: U.S. Government Printing Office, 1931–1944).

52. Allen, W. B., *George Washington: A Collection.* (Indianapolis: Liberty Classics, 1988), pp. 445–449.

53. Fitzpatrick, John C., George Washington to George Washington Parke Curtis, December 19, 1796, *The Writings of George Washington from the Original Manuscript Sources, 1745–1799*; 35:341. (Washington: U.S. Government Printing Office, 1931–1944).

54. Richardson, James D., *A Compilation of the Messages and Papers of the Presidents, 1789–1897* (Published by the authority of Congress, 1899), Vol. I, p. 220, September 17, 1796.

55. Davis, Evan, *Our Greatest President* (New York: Bedford Co. Publishers, 1891), p. 361.

56. Federer, William J., *America's God and Country Encyclopedia of Quotations.* (Coppell, TX: Fame Publishing, Inc.), pp. 204–206.

57. Lundin, Roger and Noll, Mark, *Voices from the Heart: Four Centuries of America.* (Grand Rapids, MI: Eerdman's: 1987), p. 235.

58. Hall, Verna M. and Rosalie J. Slater, The Bible and the Constitution of the United States (San Francisco: Foundation for American Christian Education, 1983), p. 27; Tim LaHaye, Faith of Our Founding Fathers (Brentwood, TN: Wolgemuth and Hyatt Publishers, Inc., 1987) pp. 76–78.

59. This section relies upon a compilation of studies and research of William J. Federer and David Barton.

60. *Church of Holy Trinity* v U.S., 143 U.S. 457 (1892).

61. Vidal v Girards Executors, 43 U.S. 126, 205 (1844).

62. People v Ruggles, 8 Johns 545, 547 (1811).

63. Berk, Herbert, *Washington's Papers* (Norristown, PA. 1907), p. 87.

The Present
NOTES

1. Staver, Matthew D., quoting D. James Kennedy, *Faith and Freedom* (Orlando, FL: Liberty Council: Orlando, 1995), XVI.

2. *School District of Abington Township v. Schempp*, 374 U.S. 203, 304 (1963).

3. *Engel v Vitale*, 370 U.S. 421 (1962) (prohibited the use of the Lord's Prayer in public schools), *School District of Abington Township vs. Schempp*, 374 U.S. 230, 304 (1963).

4. *Stone vs. Graham*, 449 U.S. 39 (1980).

5. Lapin, Rabbi Daniel, *America's Real War* (Sisters OR: Multnomah Publishers, 1999), p. 96.

6. Remarks of Martin S. Kaplan, "Survey of the Religious Right," American Jewish Committee, Board of Governors and National Counsel (September 9, 1996).

7. *Everson v Board of Education*, 330 U.S. 1, 16 (1947).

8. *McCollum v Board of Education*, 333 U.S. 203, 212 (1948).

9. *Ibid.*

10. Luther, Martin, "To the Christian Nobility of the German Nation Respecting the Reformation of the Christianist State," *Luther's Primary Works*, 162–63 (Wase and Buchheim, 1896), p. 163.

11. Oak, Dallin H., *The Wall Between Church and State* (Chicago: University of Chicago Press, 1963), p. 3.

12. Ibid.

13. Karz, Wilbur G., *Religion and American Constitutions*, Julius Rosenthal Foundation Lecture, Northwestern University School of Law, March 21, 1963.

14. Justice Anthony Kennedy characterized it as a "national theology board," *County of Allegheny v ACLU*, 492 U.S. 573 (1989).

15. *Ibid.*

16. *Wisconsin v Yoder*, 406 U.S. 205 (1972).

17. *Employment Division v Smith*, 494 U.S. 872 (1990).

18. *Church of the Lukumibabalu Aye, Inc., v City of Hialeah*, 508 U.S. 520 (1992).

19. Davis, Derek, *Original Intent* (Buffalo, NY: Promethus Books, 1991), p. 37; *Trimble v Gordon*, 430 U.S. 762 (1977).

20. Levy, Leonard W., *The Original Meaning of the Establishment Clause of the First Amendment* (Waco, TX: Baylor University Press, 1985), p. 43.

21. Bork, Robert, *The Tempting of America* (New York: The Free Press, 1990), p. 95.

22. *Lemon v Kurtzman*, 403 U.S. 602 (1971).

23. *Perry Education Association v Perry Local Educators Association*, 460 U.S. 37 (1983).

24. *Lambs Chapel vs. Center Moriches Union Free School District*, 508 U.S. 384, 393 (1993).

25. *Lee vs. Weisman*, 505 U.S. 577 (1992).
26. *Marsh vs. Chambers*, 463 U.S. 783 (1983).
27. Staver, Matthew D., *Faith and Freedom* (Liberty Counsel: Orlando, FL, 1995), pp. 83–85.
28. *Everson vs. Board of Education*, f. 7.
29. *McCollum vs. Board of Education*, f. 8.
30. *Engel vs. Vitale*, f. 3.
31. *Zorach vs. Claussen*, 343 U.S. 306 (1952).
32. *Hunt vs. McNair*, 413 U.S. 734, 741 (1973); *Mueller vs. Allen*, 463 U.S. 388 (1983).
33. *Fletcher vs. Peck,* 6 Cranch 87, 138 (1810).
34. *Barron vs. Baltimore*, 7 Peters 243, 250 (1833).
35. 310 U.S. 296 (1940), f. 7.
36. Miller, Robert T. and Flowers, Ronald B., *Toward Benevolent Neutrality: Church, State, and the Supreme Court* (Waco, TX: Markham Press, 1977), p. 5.
37. Pritchett, Charles H., *The American Constitution* (New York: McGraw-Hill, 1977), p. 32.
38. Hutchins, Robert M., *The Wall Between Church and State* (Chicago: University of Chicago Press, 1963), p. 17.
39. Howe, Mark DeWolfe, *The Garden and The Wilderness: Religion and Government in American Constitutional History* (Chicago: University of Chicago Press, 1965), pp. 136–139.
40. *Lynch vs. Donnelly*, 456 U.S. 668 (1984).
41. "Remarks by President at Prayer Breakfast," *New York Times*, August 24, 1984, A-11.
42. McDowell, Josh and Hostetler, Bob, *The New Tolerance* (Wheaton, IL: Tyndall House Publishers, 1998), p. 135.
43. Lapin, Rabbi Daniel, *America's Real War* (Sisters Oregon: Multnomah Publishers, 1999), p. 94.
44. Ibid.
45. Ibid.
46. Quoted in *Daily News*, June 14, 1986, New York Times News Service, June 13, 1986, Washington, DC, p. 1.
47. 31 *U.S.C.* 5112(d)(1).
48. 36 *U.S.C.* 186 (1956).
49. Chapter 167, 16 Stat. 168.
50. The National Gallery, Washington, D.C., exhibits more than 200 similar religious paintings.
51. *Marsh vs. Chambers*, 463 U.S. 783 (1983).

52. *Zorach vs. Claussen*, 343 U.S. 306 (1952).

53. *McGowan vs. Maryland*, 366 U.S. 420 (1961).

54. *Walz vs. Tax Commissioner*, 397 U.S. 664 (1970).

55. *Tilton vs. Richardson*, 403 U.S. 672 (1971).

56. *Church of the Holy Trinity vs. United States*, 143 U.S. 457, 468 (1892).

57. *Delaware Constitution* of 1776, Article XXII.

58. *Maryland Constitution*, 1776, Declaration of Rights, Article XXXIII.

59. *South Carolina Constitution*, 1778, Article XXXVIII.

60. *New Hampshire Constitution*, 1776, Bill of Rights, Articles V and VI.

61. Adams, Arlin N. and Emmerich, Charles J., *A Nation Dedicated to Religious Liberty* (Philadelphia: University of Pennsylvania Press, 1990), p. 14.

62. Elliott, Jay, *The Debates in the Civil State Conventions on the Adoption of the Federal Constitution*, Section 131, 2nd Edition, 1836 (May 29, 1787).

63. *Pennsylvania Constitution* of 1776, Frame of Government, Section X.

64. Miller and Flowers, f. 36.

68. Lundin, Roger and Noll, Mark, *Voices from the Heart: Four Centuries of America* (Grand Rapids: Eerdman's: 1987) p. 235.

69. Linn, William, *The Life of Thomas Jefferson* (Ithaca, NY: Mac and Andreus, 1934), p. 265.

70. Adams, Charles Francis, *The Works of John Adams, Second President of the United States* (Boston: Little, Brown, 1854), Vol. IX, 229, October 11, 1798.

71. Cousins, Norman, *In God We Trust*. (New York: Harper & Brothers, 1958), p. 42.

72. Sparks, Jared, *The Life of Gouverneur Morris* (citing "Notes on the Form of a Constitution for France") (Boston: Gray & Bowen, 1832), Vol. III, p. 48

73. Cameron, Dr. Paul, Exposing the AIDS Scandal, (Lafayette, LA: Huntington House, 1988), 11; Sowell, Thomas, The Vision of the Anointed: The Self-Congratulation as a Basis for Social Policy, (Basic Books: New York, 1995) 217. Schmidt, Alvin J., The Menace of Multiculturalism, (Preager: Westport, CT, 1997) p. 194.

74. Ibid.

Our Future
NOTES

1. Paolucci, Henry, *The Political Writings of St. Augustine* (Chicago: Gateway Editions, 1962), XXI.
2. Elliott, T. S., *Christianity in Culture* (New York: Harcourt Brace Jovanovich, 1939), p. 32.
3. Racer, David, *American Christians and Government* (St. Paul, MN: Tiny Press, 1998), ix. Introduction by Dr. Alan L. Keyes.
4. *Warsaw vs. Tehachapi*, U.S.D.C., E.D.Cal. CVF-90-404 and CVF-90-404 (1990).
5. *Roberts vs. Madigan*, 702 F.Supp. 1505 (Col. 1989); 921 F.2d 1047 (10th Cir. 1990).
6. *Commonwealth vs. Chambers*, 599 A.2d 630 (PA 1991), p. 643.
7. *Alexis deTocqueville I, Democracy in America*, 319 (1945).
8. Staver, Matthew D., *Faith and Freedom* (Liberty Counsel: Orlando, FL, 1995), pp. 444–445.
9. Robertson, Pat, *America's Dates with Destiny* (Nashville, TN: Thomas Nelson Publishers, 1986), p. 20.
10. "New York Church Loses Tax Exempt Status over Anti-Clinton Ads," Associated Press, April 1, 1999.
11. Lincoln, Abraham, "Gettysburg Address," November 19, 1863.
12. Dobson, James, *Family News*, Focus on the Family, June 1999.
13. Freund, Paul A., *Public Aid to Parochial Schools*, 82 *Harvard Law Review* 1680, 1686 (1969).
14. Joseph Cardinal Bernardin, Martin E. Marty, and Arlin M. Adams, *The Role of the Religious Leader in the Development of Public Policy*, 34 *DePaul Law Review* 1, 1984.
15. *Walz vs. Tax Commission*, 397 U.S. 664, 670 (1970).
16. Reichley, A., *Religion in Public Life*, 1985, Chapter 3, Note 23, at p. 350.
17. Bennett, William J. "Credit the Christian Right," *Washington Post*, June 26, 1994.
18. Whitehead, John W., *The Christian and Political Involvement: Responsibility of Stewardship* (Charlottesville, VA, 1992).
19. Carter, Stephen L., *The Culture of Disbelief: How American Law and Politics Trivialize Religious Devotion* (Harper Collins, 1993), p. 21.
20. Watkins, William D., *The New Absolutes* (Minneapolis, MN: Bethany House, 1996), p. 63.

21. Watkins, William D. and Fournier, Keith A., *A House Divided: Evangelicals and Catholics Together—A Winning Alliance for the Twenty-First Century* (Colorado Springs, CO: Nav Press, 1994), p. 152.
22. Lapin, Rabbi Daniel, *America's Real War* (Sisters, OR: Multnomah Publishers, 1999), p. 350.
23. Bennett, William J., *The Devaluing of America* (Colorado Springs, CO: Focus on the Family, 1992), p. 216.
24. Ezekiel 33:10.
25. Colson, Charles, *How Now Shall We Live?* (Wheaton, IL: Tyndale House Publishers, 1999), X.
26. Bates, Katharine Lee, *America the Beautiful.*
27. Reed, Ralph, *Active Faith* (New York: The Free Press, 1996), p. 24.

Additional Sources

Adair, John, Founding Fathers: The Puritans in England and America (J.M. Dent and Sons, Ltd., London, 1982).

Barton, David. Original Intent: The Courts, the Constitution, and Religion (WallBuilder Press, Aledo, TX, 1997).

Bennett, William J., The Spirit of America (Simon and Schuster, New York, NY, 1997).

Boston, Robert, Close Encounters with the Religious Right (Prometheus Books, Amherst, NY, 2000).

Boston, Robert, The Most Dangerous Man in America: Pat Robertson and The Rise of the Christian Coalition (Prometheus Books, Amherst, NY, 1996).

Bradford, M.E., Founding Fathers, 2nd Ed. (University of Kansas Press, 1981).

Bradford, William, Of Plymouth Plantation, Commonwealth of Massachusetts Edition (Wright and Porter, Boston, 1989).

Bradford, William, Of Plymouth Plantation: 1606–1646, edited by W.T. David (Charles Scribner and Sons, New York, 1908).

Bradford William, Of Plymouth Plantation: 1620–1647, edited by Samuele Morrison and Alfred A. Knopf (New York: 1952)

Collins, Alan C., The Story of America in Pictures (Doubleday and Company, Garden City, NY, 1953).

Conlin, Joseph R., The Morrow Book of Quotations and American History (Morrow and Co., New York, 1984).

Cheever, George B., Journal of the Pilgrims (John Wiley, London, 1848).

Davis, W.T., Of Plymouth Plantation, William Bradford (Charles Scribner and Sons, New York, NY, 1908).

Deetz, James and Patricia Scott, The Times of Their Lives (W.H. Freeman and Company: New York, NY, 2000).

Dexter, Henry M. Mourt's Relation, Journal of the Pilgrims, London (Henry K. Wiggin, Boston, MA, 1865).

Eidsmoe, John, Christianity and the Constitution: The Faith of Our Founding Fathers (Baker Books, Grand Rapids, MI 1987).

Gilda-Deak, Gloria, American Views: Prospects and Vistas (Viking Press: New York: NY, 1976).

MacArthur, John, The Christian and Government (Moody Press, Chicago, IL, 1986).

Marshall, Peter and Manuel, David, The Light and the Glory (Fleming H. Revel Co., Old Tappan, NJ, 1940).

Marshall, Peter and Manuel, David, Sounding Forth the Trumpet (Fleming H. Revel Co., Old Tappan, NJ, 1997).

Marshall, Peter and Manuel, David, From Sea to Shining Sea (Fleming H. Revel Co., Old Tappan, NJ, 1990).

Millard, Catherine, God's Signature Over the Nation's Capital (Son Rise Publications, New Wilmington, PA, 1985).

Morrison, Samuel E., The Oxford History of the American People (Oxford University Press: New York, NY, 1965.

Neuhaus, Richard John, The Naked Public Square: Religion and Democracy in America (Eerdmans Publishing Co., Grand Rapids, MI, 1984).

Peterson, Merrill, Jefferson: Autobiography Notes on the State of Virginia, Public and Private Papers, Addresses and Letters (University of Cambridge: 1984).

Rowe, H. Edward, Save America (Fleming H. Revell Co., Old Tappan, NJ, 1960).

Ryter, John Christian, The Baffled Christian's Handbook (R. James Bender Publishing, San Jose, CA 1996).

Scarborough, Rick, Enough is Enough: A Call to Christian Involvement, (Liberty House Publishers, Lynchburg, VA, 1996).

Schlesinger, Arthus M., Jr., The Almanac of American History (G.P. Putnam's Sons: New York, NY, 1983).

Berk, Robert, Slouching Towards Gomorrah (Regan Books, Harper Collins Publishers, New York, NY, 1996).

Smith, Christian, Christian America? What Evangelicals Really Want (University of California Press, Berkeley, CA, 2000).

The Bill of Rights: Original Meaning and Current Understanding (University Press of Virginia, Charlottesville, VA, 1991).

Thomas, Cal and Dobson, Ed, Blinded by Mights: Why the Religious Right Can't Save America (Zondervan Publishing Co., Grand Rapids, MI, 1999).

Todd, Cecil, While America Played (New Leaf Press, Green Forest, AR, 1984).

Virga, Vincent and Curators of the Library of Congress, Eyes of the Nation (Alfred A. Knopf, New York, NY, 1997).

Whitehead, John, Christians Involved in the Political Process (Moody Press, Chicago, IL, 1994).

White-Notson, Adelia and Robert Carver, Stepping Stones: The Pilgrims Own Story (Binford and Mort Publishing, Portland, OR 1987).

Whitten, Mark W., The Myth of Christian America (Smith and Helwys, Macon, GA, 1999).

"We are fools for Christ's sake and Christians must pray for courage to endure the scorn of the sophisticated world."

U.S. Supreme Court Justice Antonin Scalia (2000)

Photography © Superstock, Inc.

www.thetimefactory.com

"Without God, there is a coarsening of the society; without God, democracy will not and cannot long endure . . . America needs God more than God needs America. If we ever forget that we are One Nation Under God, then we will be a Nation gone under.

President Ronald Reagan
August 23, 1984

Our laws and our institutions must necessarily be based upon and embody the teachings of The Redeemer of mankind. It is impossible that it should be otherwise; and in this sense and to this extent our civilization and our institutions are emphatically Christian...This is a religious people. This is historically true. From the discovery of this continent to the present hour, there is a single voice making this affirmation...we find everywhere a clear recognition of the same truth...These, and many other matters which might be noticed, add a volume of unofficial declarations to the mass of organic utterances that this is a Christian nation.

SUPREME COURT DECISION, 1892.
CHURCH OF THE HOLY TRINITY V. UNITED STATES.

"A nation which does not remember what it was yesterday, does not know what it is today, nor what it is trying to do. We are trying to do a futile thing if we do not know where we came from or what we have been about."   —Woodrow Wilson

"If America is going to be safe from secular humanism, it will take the combined efforts of a pro-moral majority (the Evangelical Christian community). We must pray for the health of Christianity in America.

"If we're not the only ones interested in morality, the family, and the church—we may be the only ones motivated to speak out.

"We must inform ourselves about two religious worldviews—Christianity and Humanism with dedication on the part of the public to again live in a pro-moral America, instead of the anti-God, anti-Christian, amoral and liberal-humanist nation it is rapidly becoming."[1]

[1]Tim LaHaye, Mind Siege (Nashville, TN: Word Publishing, 2000) p. 98.

To order additional copies of

THE MYTH OF SEPARATION
BETWEEN CHURCH & STATE

Have your credit card ready and call

Toll free: (877) 421-READ (7323)

or send $19.95* each plus $5.95 S&H** to

WinePress Publishing
PO Box 428
Enumclaw, WA 98022

or order online at: www.winepressbooks.com

*WA residents, add 8.4% sales tax

**add $2.00 S&H for each additional book ordered

Dee Wampler